Pen of Iron

Pen of Iron

❦

American Prose and the
King James Bible

Robert Alter

CABRINI COLLEGE LIBRARY
610 KING OF PRUSSIA ROAD
RADNOR, PA 19087

PRINCETON UNIVERSITY PRESS
PRINCETON AND OXFORD

#373474943

Copyright © 2010 by Robert Alter

Published by Princeton University Press,
41 William Street, Princeton, New Jersey 08540
In the United Kingdom: Princeton University Press,
6 Oxford Street, Woodstock, Oxfordshire OX20 1TW
All Rights Reserved

Library of Congress Cataloging-in-Publication Data
Alter, Robert.
  American prose and the King James Bible / Robert Alter.
    p. cm.
  Includes index.
  ISBN 978-0-691-12881-8 (hardcover : alk. paper)
  1. American literature—History and criticism. 2. Bible. English—
Versions—Authorized—Influence. 3. Bible and literature. 4. Bible—
In literature. I. Title.
  PS166.A67 2010
    810.9'382—dc22
  2009022408

British Library Cataloging-in-Publication Data is available

This book has been composed in Sabon with Florens LP display

Printed on acid-free paper.
press.princeton.edu
Printed in the United States of America
10 9 8 7 6 5 4 3 2

For Dalya
a small tribute
to her great courage
and devotion

The sin of Judah *is* written with a pen of iron, *and* with the point of a diamond: *it is* graven upon the table of your heart....

—Jeremiah 17:1

Contents

∾

Acknowledgments

❧

*T*he occasion for this book was an invitation to present the Spencer Trask Lectures at Princeton University in April 2008. I am grateful for the invitation and especially appreciative of the gracious care that Hanne Winarsky of Princeton University Press devoted to making all the arrangements. I was also gratified by the generous and witty introductions I was given at the three lectures by my Princeton friends Michael Wood, Stanley Corngold, and Robert Hollander. The book itself reflects a substantial expansion of the lectures, to which I have added two additional chapters. Research expenses for this project were paid for with funds from the Class of 1937 Chair in Hebrew and Comparative Literature at the University of California at Berkeley. Janet Livingstone did an admirable job, as in the past, of converting my drafts into electronic legibility. Margarita Zaydman provided efficient and intelligent research assistance. The manuscript of the lectures was read by my dear friend, Michael Bernstein, and I am grateful for his scrupulousness as well as for his encouragement in the comments he made.

Prelude

༌

America as a Scriptural Culture

*T*he pervasiveness of the Bible in American culture from the colonial period onward has often been observed, but the fact of pervasiveness is worth recalling at the outset of this study and reframing in regard to its impact well beyond theology and creed. In England, the Protestant Reformation took an important step toward its consolidation in 1611 when the Bible was made fully accessible to the reading public in a translation that rapidly became canonical. The King James Version was famously eloquent and a beautiful instrument for conveying the vision of the biblical writers to the English- speaking populace. Its distinctive style would in the case of many major writers, beginning as early as the seventeenth century, give literary English a new and memorable coloration. (The fact that it is often inaccurate, and that the eloquence is not entirely so unflagging as most readers remember, scarcely diminishes this broad impact.) But it was in America that the potential of the 1611 translation to determine the foundational language and symbolic imagery of a whole culture was most fully realized.

The reasons for this American biblicizing impulse are

obvious enough. The Pilgrims, and their descendents for many generations, were Bible-steeped, Bible-quoting folk who saw themselves as the New Israel and the bountiful New World they had entered as the Promised Land. (One famous expression of this mind-set was that when Harvard College was founded in 1636, Hebrew was a required language for all first-year students.[1]) This identification with biblical Israel meant that it was the Old Testament far more than the New that was the biblical text of reference. (Harvard required Hebrew but not *koine* Greek.) The American landscape was dotted with towns bearing the names of ancient Israelite places—Salem, Bethel, Bethlehem, Shiloh—as though the New World were a reincarnation of Canaan. The anchorage of Hebrew Scripture in ideas of family, nationhood, land, and politics spoke to the early settlers and their descendents in a way that the New Testament could not easily do. To put this differently, the Hebrew Bible was pervaded by a sense of national destiny deeply engaged in history, whereas the New Testament addressed individuals in urgent need of salvation as the kingdom—which is to say, the end of history—was about to come. It was the outlook of the Hebrew writers more than that of their Christian successors that seemed compellingly relevant to the American situation. Mark A. Noll has noted that on Washington's death, just seven of the 120 biblical texts cited in the published eulogies were drawn from the New Testament, and four of those seven referred to Old Testament characters.[2]

---

[1] Shalom Goldman offers a scrupulous account of the American romance with the Hebrew language in *God's Sacred Tongue: Hebrew and the American Imagination* (Chapel Hill: University of North Carolina Press, 2004).

[2] Mark A. Noll, "The United States as a Biblical Nation," in *The Bible in*

What I should like to emphasize in regard to the American novelists from the nineteenth century to the twenty-first whom I shall be considering is that the language of the Old Testament in its 1611 English version continued to suffuse the culture even when the fervid faith in Scripture as revelation had begun to fade. There were, of course, other significant strands of American literary English, and in the case of some major writers, the traces of the biblical background are almost entirely absent, whether because the writer is cultivating a colloquial vein (signally initiated by Mark Twain) or elaborating a language of nuance and conceptual discrimination altogether unlike anything biblical (Henry James being the exemplary instance of this stylistic direction). Yet the language of the Bible remains an ineluctable framework for verbal culture in this country. Edmund Wilson, who at the beginning of his sixth decade took the trouble to study biblical Hebrew, evocatively describes the presence of the language of the Bible in our culture.

> Here it is, that old tongue, with its clang and its flavor, sometimes rank, sometimes sweet, sometimes bitter; here it is in its concise solid stamp. Other cultures have felt its impact, and none—in the West, at least—seems quite to accommodate to it. Yet we find we have been living with it all our lives.[3]

Wilson emphasizes the resonant sound and the distinctive feel of the language of the Bible, but he intimates something else as well: that this language articulates a

America, edited by Nathan O. Hatch and Mark A. Noll (New York: Oxford University Press, 1982), p. 45.

[3]Edmund Wilson, *A Piece of My Mind* (Garden City: Doubleday Anchor Books, 1958), p. 88.

set of values, or perhaps one should say, a set of demands, and a way of imagining man, God, and history, with which we must wrestle, and which we perhaps never quite succeed in fitting to the shape of our own world. In this regard, the Bible as a foundational text of Western literature differs from the Greek and Latin classics because of the sense of moral or spiritual imperative that it imposes. The story of the powerful afterlife of the Bible in the prose style of American fiction is a prime instance of how any verbal culture remains dialogically engaged with its own earlier strata. In the evolution of culture, and perhaps verbal culture in particular, very little is altogether discarded. Once a text, together with the language in which it is cast, has been authoritative, that authority continues to make its force felt in the work of later writers, even those who no longer assent to the original grounds for the authority. This dynamic is by no means limited to religious texts. Homer is the defining model of epic poetry in the Western tradition. Virgil is inconceivable without him, and after Virgil, Tasso, Milton, even a good deal of Pope, and, then, transmogrified into prose, Joyce. American writers continued to perceive in the language of the Bible certain qualities of powerful eloquence, paradoxically coupled with a homespun simplicity ("its concise solid stamp") that they wanted to draw on as resources in their own writing. At the same time, one must remember that style is not merely a constellation of aesthetic properties but is the vehicle of a particular vision of reality. Those American writers who wove into their prose elements of the language of the Bible could scarcely ignore what the sundry biblical texts were saying about the world, and so they were often impelled to argue with the canonical text, or to tease out dissident views within the biblical corpus, or sometimes to reaffirm its conception of things, or to place biblical terms in new contexts that could be surprising or even unsettling.

Typically, moreover, the writers were arguing not just with the Bible itself but with a body of interpretation of the Bible, inserting their own readings into what amounted to a hermeneutical debate. Some American writers have explicitly deployed biblical motifs and references to specific biblical texts, but that will not be my main concern in what follows, and consequently I will be engaged only incidentally in the tracking of allusions to the Bible. In any case, previous scholarship has done that, at least for Melville and Faulkner. And it is also well to keep in mind that an immersion in the Bible does not invariably manifest itself in style, which is the focus of this study. African-American culture, for example, has been famously steeped in the Bible, and so I initially assumed that Ralph Ellison's *Invisible Man*, one of the major American novels of the mid-twentieth century, would be perfect for my inquiry, but unfortunately a renewed inspection of its prose revealed only oblique and episodic links with biblical style. Rather than tracing the "influence" of the Bible on American writers, I should like to try to see how the language of the King James Version is worked into the texture of the writing, making possible a kind of strong prose that would not have existed otherwise, and I shall seek to understand how this prose serves as the vehicle for certain distinctively American constructions of reality. There are admirable scholarly studies of the powerful presence of the Bible in American culture, from Sacvan Bercovitch to Nancy Rutenberg, that devote particular attention to biblical theology, symbols, and ideas, but what I want to focus on here is how the canonical English translation of the Bible, itself an impressive stylistic achievement, made a difference in style for certain major American novelists.

Serious writing in this country—what these days is unfortunately called "literary fiction"—has been both a deep sharer of popular perceptions of the Bible and strenuously—at times, subversively—critical of them. The Bible is surely not ubiquitous in American culture as it once was (and current ignorance of the fundamental biblical texts is notoriously widespread), yet Scripture, now in a variety of English versions, continues to sell millions of copies in this country, and polls continue to show that as many as 85% of Americans view it as the revealed word of God. It is hard to know what to make of such statistics because one may wonder whether many people respond to the pollster's question by stating not necessarily what they believe but what they think they ought to believe. My guess is that beyond evangelical circles, which of course are by no means numerically inconsequential, only a small minority shares the absolute faith of the early Puritans in Scripture as literal divine revelation. Yet the novelists I will be considering register in their work a sense about the Bible that "we have been living with it all our lives." Some of them grew up in devout homes but almost none remained devout. In every case I will consider but one, there is a perceptible distance between the writer and biblical values, but the result is not simple rejection. It is easy to assume the stance of the village atheist if you think only of ideology or theology, as several recent anti-religious polemicists have done. An imaginative writer, on the other hand, is before all else a language-using animal, and when the language of the texts you cannot embrace as revealed truth is strongly chiseled, hewn from deep quarries of moral and spiritual experience, you somehow have to contend with it and, given its intrinsic poetic power, you may even be tempted to put it to use. That contending, and those various uses, will be the subject of this inquiry.

Chapter 1

ꝏ

Style in America and the
King James Version

*A*s I assemble these reflections on the presence of the
King James Version in American writing, the fourth centennial of the 1611 translation stands on the horizon. A
great deal has changed in American culture since the
third centennial was celebrated in 1911. At that juncture, the King James Version was extolled by leading
public figures such as Theodore Roosevelt and Wood-
row Wilson as America's national book and as the text
that more than any other had affected the life of English-
speaking peoples. My guess is that the 2011 milestone
will be marked more in academic circles than in the public domain. In the century since the previous centennial
was celebrated, two major shifts have taken place: the
practice of reading the Bible aloud, of reading the Bible
at all, and of memorizing passages from the Bible has
drastically diminished; and the King James Bible has
ceased to be the almost universally used translation as
readers have been encouraged to use more "accessible"

versions, which also happen to be stylistically inferior in virtually all respects.

The decline of the role of the King James Version in American culture has taken place more or less simultaneously with a general erosion of a sense of literary language, although I am not suggesting a causal link. The reasons for this latter development have often been noted, and hence the briefest summary will suffice for the purpose of the present argument: Americans read less, and read with less comprehension; hours once devoted to books from childhood on are more likely to be spent in front of a television set or a computer screen; epistolary English, once a proving ground for style, has been widely displaced by the high-speed short-cut language of e-mail and text-messaging. The disappearance of a sense of style even makes itself felt in popular book reviewing. Most contemporary reviewers clearly have no tools to discuss style, or much interest in doing so. One unsettling symptom of the general problem is that in the country's most influential reviewing platform, the *New York Times Book Review*, when a critic singles out a writer for stylistic brilliance, it is far more often than not the case that the proffered illustrative quotation turns out to be either flat and banal writing or prose of the most purple hue. Obviously, there are still people in the culture, including young people, who have a rich and subtle sense of language, but they are an embattled minority in a society where tone-deafness to style is increasingly prevalent. That tone-deafness has also affected the academic study of literature, but there are other issues involved in the university setting, and to those I shall turn in due course.

In sharp contrast to our current condition, American

culture in the mid-nineteenth century, where my considerations of the biblical strand in the novel begin, cultivated the adept use of language in a variety of ways. The
relish for language was by no means restricted to high
culture: the vigor and wit of the American vernacular
were prized qualities that were widely exercised, and
one can see their literary transmutation in the prose of
Mark Twain and the poetry of Walt Whitman and Emily
Dickinson. The thorough familiarity in this period with
the strong and eloquent language of the King James
Bible provided an important resource, beyond the vital
inventiveness of spoken American English, that nour-
ished the general sense of style.

A case in point is the prose of one of the finest stylists
of nineteenth-century America, Abraham Lincoln. He
was, we recall, a man who had virtually no formal school-
ing. Just as he taught himself law through his own studi-
ous efforts, he developed a powerful and nuanced sense
of English through his own reading. It is not easy to
imagine comparable instances in our own time in which
such mastery of language could be acquired through the
sheer dedication of an autodidact. The force of Lincoln's
speeches derives from a number of different sources, one
of which was biblical. He had a wonderful native sense
for the expressive use of cadence, repetition, antithesis,
and for the cinching effectiveness of a periodic sentence.
Especially in the formal architecture of his speeches, he
also registered the influence of oratory inspired by the
American Greek Revival.[1] At times the persuasive force

[1] On the background of the Greek Revival, see Garry Wills, *Lincoln at Gettysburg* (New York: Simon and Schuster, 1992), pp. 41–62. A more elaborate and probing stylistic analysis of the Gettysburg Address is offered

of his public rhetoric was altogether lawyerly, which is hardly surprising. His First Inaugural Address, for example, deploys lawyerly language from one end to the other because it is an argument to the nation on the question of whether there is a right of secession and whether the Union can continue without civil war. "If the United States be not a government proper, but an association of States in the nature of contract only, can it, as a contract, be peaceably unmade by less than all the parties who made it?" Here, as throughout the Address, one hears the voice of Lincoln the Illinois lawyer, sorting out in plain and precise language issues of contract and constitution and consent as the Republic faced a fateful juncture. This language, too, is a kind of rhetoric. The stylistic plainness, as Gary Wills, looking at Lincoln's revisions, has shown,[2] is a quality that Lincoln labored to perfect over time, especially against a background of American oratory that favored highly wrought ornamentation.

We more typically remember Lincoln's speeches for their eloquence. Much of this, as I have suggested, is achieved through his intuitive feel for appropriate diction and rhythmic emphasis, manifested, most famously, in every phrase of the Gettysburg Address, as in the grand concluding sweep of "we here highly resolve that these dead shall not have died in vain," moving on to the climactic anaphora, "that government of the people, by the people, for the people, shall not perish from the earth." Only a single phrase in the Address is explicitly

by Stephen Booth in *Precious Nonsense* (Berkeley: University of California Press, 1998).

[2]Wills, *Lincoln at Gettysburg*, especially pp. 157–60.

biblical, though one might argue that the very use of a language that is both plain and dignified, resonant in its very ordinariness, is in part inspired by the diction of the King James Version. Many people, I suspect, assume that the opening phrase, "Four score and seven years ago," is explicitly biblical, though in fact it is merely modeled on the "three score and ten" of the King James Version, a phrase that, given the sacred status of the formulaic number seventy, appears 111 times in the 1611 translation. The Hebrew actually has no equivalent expression and simply says "seventy," as does Tyndale's translation, which was a principal source for the King James translators. Their decision to use this compound form would seem to reflect a desire to give their version a heightened and deliberately archaic flourish (it seems unlikely that this is the way ordinary Englishmen said "seventy" in the seventeenth century), and Lincoln clearly responded to this aim in adopting the form. The difference between "eighty-seven" and "four score and seven" is that the former is a mere numerical indication whereas the latter gives the passage of time since the founding of the Republic weight and solemnity. This effect in part is a consequence of breaking the number into two pieces, forcing us to slow down as we take it in and compute it. But it also has something to do with the archaic character of the phrase, and in this regard the background of the King James Version has a direct relevance. The 1611 translation, as has often been observed, was in general a little archaic even in its own time. By the middle decades of the nineteenth century, much of its language was surely felt to be archaic (and even then, perhaps not always perfectly understood), and yet the text was, paradoxically, part of everyday life, a familiar fixture of hearth and home. In this way, the sheer dissemination of the King James Version created a stylistic precedent for the American ear in which a language that was elaborately old-fashioned, that stood at a distance from contemporary usage, was assumed to be the vehicle for expressing matters of high import and grand spiritual scope. Thus, "four score and seven years ago," a biblicizing phrase that is not an actual quotation, sounds a strong note of biblical authority at the beginning of the Gettysburg Address.

The concluding flourish, by contrast, "shall not perish from the earth," is a direct citation from the Bible. It appears three times, always without the "not," and only in the Hebrew Bible: "His remembrance shall perish from the earth" (Job 18:17); "The gods that have not made the heavens and the earth, even they shall perish from the earth" (Jeremiah 10:11); "The good man is perished out of the earth" (Micah 7:2). (Although the 1611 translation uses a different preposition for the verse from Micah, the original uses the same preposition, *min*, "from," in all three cases.) The borrowing of the biblical phrase is not really an allusion to a particular scriptural intertext but rather the use, in the perorational final gesture of the Address, of a familiar biblical idiom that gives the speaker's own language the breadth and moral gravity of the Bible. The Bible begins with God's creation of heaven and earth. It includes repeated grim intimations, both in this particular phrasing and related ones, of individuals, nations, humankind perishing from the earth, wiped out from the face of the earth. The idea of persisting in or desisting from existence is given, one could say, a cosmic perspective and a certain precariousness in the biblical language. Imagine the different effect if Lincoln had concluded his speech with a phrase like "shall not come to an end" or "shall not cease to exist." The meaning would have been approximately the same, but the sense of magnitude, the idea of the nation realizing a new and hopeful destiny "under God," as Lincoln wrote, would have been diminished. The sternly grand language of the King James Bible, as Melville had already demonstrated more than a decade earlier and as Faulkner and others would demonstrate in different ways later, was a way of giving American English a reach and resonance it would otherwise not have had.

Lincoln's greatest speech besides the Gettysburg Address is his Second Inaugural Address. It begins by affirming that the historical moment—the Union in still tense expectation on the verge of successfully concluding four years of bloody conflict—invites brevity. It is in fact a fifth the length of the First Inaugural Address (though still twice as long as the breathtakingly concise Gettysburg Address). The first half of the speech, into the middle of the third of its four paragraphs, is a factual review of the course of the war and its origins in the dispute over slavery. There is nothing biblical in this first section. Instead, Lincoln displays his ability to use plain and precise language—for example, "To strengthen, perpetuate, and extend this interest [of slavery] was the object for which the insurgents would rend the Union even by war." His gift for emphatic antithesis in succinct parallel clauses is also in evidence here. The Bible is explicitly mentioned at the midpoint of the Address: "Both read the same Bible and pray to the same God, and each invokes His aid against the other." (One wonders whether in this wry awareness of the competing uses to which Scripture and deity are put Lincoln may have been remembering the passage from Voltaire's *Candide* in which both warring armies celebrate a Te Deum to thank God for permitting them to destroy their enemies.) Once the Bible has been introduced in this fashion, biblical quotations and weighted phrases drawn from the language of the Bible are predominant for the rest of the Address. "It may seem strange," Lincoln now goes on to say, "that any men should dare to ask a just God's assistance in wringing their bread from the sweat of other men's faces, but let us judge not, that we may not be judged." The first clause, of course, gives a vigorous homiletic twist to God's curse of Adam in Genesis 3:19, pointedly and concisely suggesting that slavery is a fundamental perversion of the divine moral order. The second clause, a slightly modified quotation of Luke 6:37, strikes at least a rhetorical balance in a gesture of conciliation to the South (though it is hard to dismiss that telling image of wringing bread from the sweat of other men's faces). The verse from Luke occurs in the midst of the Beatitudes and immediately after the injunction to "love your enemies," so we can see how Lincoln is making the utmost use of his scriptural sources with a kind of preacherly canniness. The only other explicit quotation from the Bible appears at the end of the extraordinary sentence that concludes this long paragraph:

> Yet if God wills that it [the war] continue until all the wealth piled up by the bondsman's two hundred and fifty years of unrequited toil shall be sunk, and until

every drop of blood drawn by the lash shall be paid by another drawn by the sword, as was said three thousand years ago, so still it must be said, "the judgments of the Lord are true and righteous together."

As we shall have occasion to see, Faulkner, too, will use biblicizing language to represent the full historical gravity of the sin of slavery, linking the bloodshed of slavery to Cain's murder of his brother Abel. "Lash" is a very immediate synecdoche for the violence perpetrated through slavery, whereas "sword"—one again observes the power of Lincoln's antitheses—is a reiterated biblical synecdoche for warfare. The citation of Psalm 19:9 about the judgments of the Lord strongly affirms that the devastation of the slave states is an act of divine retribution. ("Let us judge not, that we may not be judged" is no longer much in evidence here.) Elsewhere, the second half of the Address is punctuated by biblical locutions that are not quite quotations. American slavery is said to have been permitted by God to continue through "His appointed time." "The appointed time" is an often recurring biblical idiom, especially in Hebrew Scripture and particularly in the Prophets, where it indicates the unfolding of a divine plan in human events. A few lines later, Lincoln writes, "Fondly do we hope, fervently do we pray, that this mighty scourge of war may speedily pass away." The first two clauses vividly illustrate the effectiveness of parallelism in Lincoln's rhetoric. The "scourge" of war is a strongly expressive biblicism: it is a word that occurs in a variety of biblical contexts, almost never in its literal sense of "whip," but, as here, in the metaphorical sense of devastating punishment. The concluding phrase "may speedily pass away" does not occur as a collocation in the Bible, but both "speedily" and "pass away" are biblicisms that, coupled with "this mighty scourge of war," give the whole clause its strength. (Again, had Lincoln written "rapidly" instead of "speedily," much of the effect would have been lost.) Finally, the brief one-sentence paragraph that ends the Address begins with another of Lincoln's splendid parallelisms, "With malice towards none, with charity for all," and then moves into two additional biblical locutions, "to bind up the nation's wounds" and "to care for him who shall have borne the battle and for his widow and his orphans." The addition of "up" to "bind" gives the verb a biblical coloration, evoking, without specific allusion, a variety of prophetic promises of healing and restoration. And though it may seem perfectly logical to mention the widow and orphans of the man fallen in battle, this, too, is a collocation that occurs again and again in the Hebrew Bible as exemplary instances of those who are helpless and in need of support.

Lincoln's prose powerfully illustrates the semantic depth and stylistic gravity that American novelists as well would often tap in drawing on the language of the King James Bible. His writing, as we have seen, is by no means pervasively biblical, but at the appropriate junctures it mobilizes biblical diction both to effect a stylistic heightening and to bring into play an element of moral or explicitly theological vision. The grand concluding movement of the Second Inaugural Address aims to engage the audience in a vision of justice and healing and peace after four years of devastating warfare, and the vehicle that makes this possible is the language of the

Bible. At a cultural moment when the biblical text, verse and chapter, was a constant presence in American life, the idioms and diction and syntax incised in collective memory through the King James translation became a wellspring of eloquence.

Eloquence, of course, is an attribute we readily associate with oratory, but not with the novel. The prominence of biblical motifs or allusions in certain major American novelists has often been observed, but what I should like to consider is whether the language of the English Bible made a difference in the texture of the prose, enabling crucial shifts or heightenings of perspective, as it did in Lincoln's speeches. The general insistence of this inquiry on the importance of style may itself seem anachronistic to some, a mere indulgence in an aesthetic aspect of prose fiction that is of dubious relevance to what novels are really about, and so a few comments are in order about the role of style in fiction.

Does style in the novel in fact count for much? The evidence of the novelists themselves is somewhat mixed. A few prominent novelists, such as Dreiser, have been wretched stylists. Trollope's prose was no more than serviceable, yet with it he produced an abundance of genuinely engaging novels, a good many of which are fine representations of class and character in Victorian England. Balzac was not at all a brilliant stylist, and on occasion he could be bombastic, especially in his handling of figurative language, but *The Human Comedy* is among the most grand and enduring achievements of the genre. Stendhal famously announced that he wanted to fashion a factual, understated prose that would compete with the language of the civil registry, but style makes a difference in his novels, and anyone who has read him in French is likely to sense a sad diminution of his lightness of touch and his worldly tone in the English translations. At the other end of the spectrum, many great novelists have been exquisite, and in some cases, painstaking, stylists: Fielding (whom Stendhal greatly admired); Flaubert, the inaugurator of the modern idea of the novelist as fastidious artificer; Joyce, Kafka, and Nabokov, all of them in varying ways emulating the model of Flaubert; and, among many possible American instances, Melville, a wildly energetic improviser whose prose we shall consider in detail, and Henry James, whose stylistic disposition is in its idiosyncratic way Flaubertian rather than biblical.

The question of style in the novel that animates the present study urgently needs to be addressed because it has been so widely neglected, especially in academic circles, since the 1970s. More recently, there have been some encouraging signs of a renewed interest in close reading and the formal aspects of literature, but the legacy of the neglect of style is still with us. The principal reason for this neglect is quite evident: in departments of literary studies, the very term and concept of style— even of language itself—have been frequently displaced by what is usually referred to as discourse, a notion that chiefly derives from Michel Foucault. Discourse in the sense that has generally been adopted is a manifestation, or perhaps rather a tool, of ideology. It flows through the circuits of society, manipulating individuals and groups in the interests of the powers that be, manifesting itself equally, or at least in related ways, in fiction and in poetry, in political speeches, government directives, manuals of mental and physical hygiene, advertising, and much else. This orientation toward discourse was at the heart of the New Historicism (now a fading phenomenon), and it is instructive that one of its founders, Stephen Greenblatt, in the preface to his admirable *Hamlet in Purgatory*, should have felt constrained to say that there is no point in talking about Shakespeare if you do not respond to the magic of the language, thus implicitly repudiating many of his followers and perhaps some of his own earlier inclinations.

After the New Historicism, though sometimes drawing on it, at least indirectly, literary scholars have been busy pursuing a variety of purportedly political agendas with sometimes no more than illustrative reference to literary texts—race, class, gender identity, sexual practices, the critique of colonialism, the excoriation of consumerism and of the evils of late capitalism and globalization. There has scarcely been room in such considerations for any attention to style, for the recognition that it is literary style that might make available to us certain precious perceptions of reality and certain distinctive pleasures not to be found elsewhere. When one encounters intelligent appreciations of style these days, they tend to come from practicing novelists, or from a few critics who have no more than one foot in academic life.

There is, let me hasten to say, no logical contradiction between attention to style and attention to ideology. At least in the more extreme instances of ideologically motivated writing, virtually the opposite is true. Ideology may impel a writer to certain stylistic choices—or, since this is a chicken-and-egg phenomenon, the fondness for certain stylistic gestures may conceivably predispose a writer to embrace a particular ideology. There are certainly cases in which stylistic analysis could illuminate the role of ideology in a literary work in fresh and instructive ways. Thus, the fascinating Hebrew modernist poet Uri Zvi Greenberg (1896–1981), who became a militant Zionist extremist and a kind of Jewish racist, deploys a wild and disruptively aggressive language in his strongest poems from the 1920s onward that is intimately connected with his politics, and a just account of such a writer would have to consider style and ideology together. Greenberg has clear affinities with German Expressionism (born in the Hapsburg Empire, he absorbed German as his first European language after his native Yiddish), and if one recalls that the eminent Expressionist poet, Gottfried Benn, was at least until 1936 an ardent supporter of Nazism, some correspondence between the Expressionist aesthetic and fascist values may be worth investigating. Most writers have views on political questions, even if such views are no more than obliquely implicit in their work, and I am not suggesting that either the implied or the explicit politics of a writer should be ignored. What has happened too often, however, in American literary studies is that the focus on ideological considerations has tended to reduce the literary work to its inferable propositional content, the analysis, bent on "unmasking" the text, looking past the articulations of style that are compellingly interesting in their own right and that might in fact complicate the understanding of the propositional content. The claim I make in this study for the importance of style is not an attempt to cut off literature from its moorings in history and politics but rather an argument that we will be better served by looking with a finer focus at the very linguistic medium writers use to engage with history and politics and perhaps in some instances to transform our vision of both those realms.

A recent book that does concentrate on style in the novel is Adam Thirlwell's *The Delighted States*.[3] Thirlwell, a young British novelist who has read widely and enthusiastically in several languages, lays out a playful tour through the history of the novel that has considerable charm and poses some important questions about style in the novel, even if it is not altogether conceptually satisfying in the answers it provides. Although the descriptive flourish of Thirlwell's lengthy comic subtitle mentions "four continents" as the setting for this story about the novel, his attention is mainly devoted to European writers, with the United States represented only by Saul Bellow (unless one wants to allow Nabokov as an American writer). One reason for the particular engagement in European—and to a lesser extent, Latin American—novelists is that they exhibit more to-and-fro movement from culture to culture, usually through the agency of translation, than one finds among North American writers, and the question of novels in translation is at the heart of Thirlwell's book. Its most valuable contribution to the discussion of style in the novel is to have put forth the phenomenon of translation as a kind of test case about the role of style in fiction.

[3]Adam Thirlwell, *The Delighted States: A Book of Novels, Romances, and Their Unknown Translators, Containing Ten Languages, Set on Four Continents, and Accompanied by Maps, Portraits, Squiggles, Illustrations, and a Variety of Helpful Indexes* (New York: Farrar, Straus and Giroux, 2008).

Novels are famously, or perhaps notoriously, translatable. That very translatability poses a challenge to anyone who thinks, as I do, that lexical nuances and patterns of sound and subtleties of syntax are crucial to the sense of reality articulated in novels. There is something scandalous, Thirlwell suggests, though he does not use that term, about the manifest translatability of the novel. Let me mention two rather different examples that he also invokes, *Don Quixote* and *Madame Bovary*. I would assume that what linguistically informed readers characterize as the pungency and energy of Cervantes' Spanish is not fully conveyed by any of his translators, and yet *Don Quixote* has had an immensely fructifying effect on many different English, French, German, Russian, and Yiddish novelists whose only access to it was through translation. Perhaps this is not altogether surprising. The arresting archetypes of the endearingly daft emaciated Don and his pragmatic roly-poly sidekick grab the imagination, even when the language of the translation may be a somewhat anemic approximation of the original. But the other novel in question that has had a widespread effect on later writers is *Madame Bovary* (which of course itself displays Cervantes' paradigm of a delusional sense of reality imbibed through reading). Flaubert, unlike Cervantes, is a novelist fanatically devoted to stylistic refinements, aspiring to a prose, as he says in one of his letters, that will perform the high function in literary culture that was once the domain of poetry. Nevertheless, even with many of these refinements scarcely visible in the sundry translations, this story of the frustrated wife of a provincial doctor, her two disastrous love affairs, and her suicide has been compelling for countless readers and has given many writers a strong precedent for their own fiction.

There is a tricky balance between the sheer weight of the represented world of a novel and the force of the language in which it is conveyed. Novels, one must concede, are urgently about a whole variety of things that are not made up of words: events, individual character, relationships, institutions, social forces, historical movements, material culture, and much more. If the translator inevitably substitutes other words, and usually less adequate ones, than the novelist's to point to all these disparate elements of the represented fictional world, the mere act of pointing often proves to be efficacious enough. There are no doubt all sorts of effects in the Russian of *Anna Karenina* that are lost on those of us who read it in English, yet when we follow Kitty, in the company of her mother, on her way up the grand staircase to her first ball, we get a perfectly vivid sense of her delighted self-consciousness in her own appearance, the sound of the orchestra filtering down from the ballroom, the parade of people in formal dress on the stairs, and the general excitement of the moment. Tolstoy's subtle handling of the narrative point of view, his wonderfully strategic choice of descriptive detail, and his ability to enter so convincingly into Kitty's thoughts and feelings, all make this possible, and none of it is strictly dependent on language.

Yet something happens in novels through the elaborately wrought medium of style that resists translation, even as the large represented world of the novel is conveyed well enough in another language. How that "something" manifests itself in the American novel through a biblical inflection will be the subject of the chapters that follow. A second issue of translation is involved in this question of American prose style. The King James Version is itself a translation, one in which some of the contours of English were reshaped mainly in accordance with a Hebrew original. Though I can attest that reading Genesis or Job in the 1611 translation is by no means the same as reading it in the Hebrew, much from the themes and imagery and characterization of the Hebrew is nevertheless preserved, and has deeply affected untold numbers of English readers, among them major writers. A language stretched and bent for the purposes of translation thus became a primary model of English style that American writers in particular have been drawn to embrace. But if translation can be the engine of stylistic creativity, merely competent (or less than competent) translation as a vehicle for conveying the represented world of the fiction has the effect of diluting or obscuring many of the most deeply engaging aspects of the original.

Let me propose a partial list of attributes of style that make a difference in our experience of the work of fiction, that generally resist translation, and that are neglected in literary studies to the peril of our understanding of literature. These are: sound (rhythm, alliteration, assonance, and so forth), syntax, idiomatic usage and divergences from it, linguistic register (that is, level of diction), and the cultural and literary associations of language. I would like to consider some instances of how these attributes of style make themselves felt in fiction, keeping in mind the instructive test of translatability. My initial examples are from Melville, to whom I shall direct more sustained attention in the next chapter.

If you try to imagine *Moby-Dick* in French or Chinese or Hindi, you can readily conceive that the tale of Ahab's monstrous monomania and of the exotic crew of the *Pequod*, the tremendous evocations of the great white whale as a virtually mythological presence, would all come across to far-flung readers in different languages. All this constitutes what I have referred to as the represented world of the novel, the powerfully imagined material of fictional mimesis. This represented world, as I noted in connection with Tolstoy, is not entirely dependent on the language in which it is conveyed, and one may grant the contention of many theorists of the novel that it is the represented world that is primary. But if style is in some sense secondary, it nevertheless has electrifying importance, as I shall try to illustrate. Consider even a brief sentence from Melville's novel: "The sea was as a crucible of molten gold, that bubblingly leaps with light and heat."[4] A translation could easily reproduce the simile of molten gold and the vigor of the verb "leaps," but the deliberate oddness of the adverbial "bubblingly" that focuses, by a small swerve from established English usage, the movement of the water, and the alliteration and assonance of "leaps with light and heat" that lock the clause together—these are another matter. All these small stylistic effects help create the lyric intensity of this moment of the sea perceived from the moving ship, and they would necessarily be diminished in translation. They constitute what Stephen Greenblatt calls the magic of the language, and that to a large degree is what makes the experience of reading this book so mesmerizing.

[4]Herman Melville, *Moby-Dick* (New York: W. W. Norton, 1967), p. 423.

A different operation of the force of style may be seen in these words from a dramatic monologue by the black cabin-boy Pip. Here, as so often in Melville, characteristics of the canonical English Bible come into play together with other elements of style: "Oh, thou big white God aloft there somewhere in yon darkness, have mercy on this small black boy down here; preserve him from all men that have no bowels to fear!" (p. 155). The artful shaping of the language may be less spectacular in this sentence than in the previous one quoted, but it is no less decisive. The dense cluster of monosyllabic words generates a clenched power. Instead of any gesture toward African-American dialect, Pip is made to speak a high-register poetic language that in its pronounced iambic cadences is reminiscent, like much else in this novel, of Shakespeare. (In the lines just before the words I have quoted, Pip utters disjointed syllables that sound rather like the Fool in *Lear*.) The archaic "yon" is ancillary to this Shakespearian impulse, though at the same time it may be nautical language, like "aloft." The use of "bowels" in the sense of "deep feelings" or "compassion" is drawn directly from the King James Version, where the word appears as a literal rendering of a Hebrew idiom, and like the hints of Shakespeare, it points back to the early seventeenth century. The high solemnity of Pip's address to God could presumably be conveyed in a language other than English, but it is the specific biblical resonances (perhaps especially of Psalms) and also those of Shakespeare (as usual in this novel, especially pointing to *Lear*) that give these words their peculiar metaphysical dignity.

Let us look at a more elaborate example from *Moby-*

Dick in which repetition of sound, poetic rhythm, and interplay of dictions with reminiscences of the Bible are beautifully orchestrated. Here are the last three paragraphs of Ahab's apostrophe first to savage nature and then to a dying whale that occurs late in the novel (chapter 116).

"Oh, thou dark Hindoo half of nature, who of drowned bones has built thy separate throne somewhere in the heart of these unverdured seas; thou art an infidel, thou queen, and too truly speakest to me in the wide-slaughtering Typhoon, and the hushed burial of its after calm. Nor has this thy whale sunwards turned his head without a lesson to me.

"Oh, trebly hooped and welded hip of power! Oh, high aspiring rainbow jet!—that one striveth, this one jetteth all in vain! In vain, oh whale, dost thou seek intercedings with yon all-quickening sun, that only calls forth life, but gives it not again. Yet dost thou, darker half, rock me with a prouder, if a darker faith. All thy unnamable imminglings float beneath me here; I am buoyed by breaths of once living things, exhaled as ash, but water now.

"Then hail, for ever hail, O sea, in whose eternal tossings the wild fowl finds his only rest. Born of earth, yet suckled by the sea, though hill and valley mothered me, ye billows are my foster-brothers." (pp. 409–10)

The language of Ahab's elevated speech is all at once, or alternately, Shakespearian, Miltonic, and biblical. Some of the turns of formal apostrophe sound more like the epic invocations of the muse in *Paradise Lost* than like anything in Shakespeare ("Then hail, for ever hail").

The formal poetic character of the passage is strongly reinforced by the iambic cadences it repeatedly uses—"and then gone round again," "Oh, trebly hooped and welded hip of power," "that only calls forth life, but gives it not again." Syntactic inversion is another marker of poetic formality—"this thy whale sunwards turned his dying head," "Yet dost thou." Alliteration under-scores the emphatic force of the language—"Hindoo half," "bones... builded," "buoyed by breath," "hooped hip." (The use of "Hindoo" as an adjective illustrates Melville's disposition to turn references to the exotic into rhetorical terms—here, the word referring to what is alien, unknown, inscrutable—perhaps, as some have suggested, with Kali, the goddess of destruction, in mind.) The invented adjective "unverdured" is probably a con-scious emulation of Shakespeare, who, for example, coined the verb "incarnadine" in *Macbeth*. The archaic verbal form "builded," on the other hand, is a borrow-ing from the King James Version, as, most memorably, in Proverbs 9:1, "Wisdom has builded her house, she has hewn out her seven pillars." Equally biblical is the fond-ness for semantically parallel clauses—a stylistic trait that we will explore in greater detail in the next chap-ter—as in "that one striveth, this one jetteth all in vain." ("Strive" in particular is a recurrent term in the biblical lexicon.) "Hip," because it is linked to "power," proba-bly recalls the biblical "he smote them, hip and thigh with a giant slaughter" (Judges 15:8). Counterpointed to the taut, intermittently biblical diction are two poly-syllabic and abstract word choices—"intercedings" and the wonderfully alliterative coinage, "unnamable im-minglings." The concluding sweep of Ahab's apostrophe significantly invokes reminiscences of the Bible without actual allusion. The "wild fowl" shows a trace of "the fowl of the air" of the Creation story in Genesis 1. "Born of the earth yet suckled by the sea" is a neat replication of antithetical parallelism in biblical poetry (with the first phrase also pointing to the making of the first human in Genesis 2), while "finds his only rest" recalls a variety of biblical locutions involving rest and resting place. Finally, the "billows" are King James language for "waves," as in Jonah's psalm (Jonah 2:3), "all thy billows and thy waves passed over me." In all this, one palpably feels that the *texture* of Melville's language is decisive in shaping what he wants to say about the whale, the sea, the natural world, and the finally anti-biblical nature of reality as he conceives it.

To apply the test of translatability one last time, it is instructive to compare Melville's prose here with a recent French version. The French is elegant, idiomatically smooth, and in most respects relatively accurate. It does a good job in catching the formal side of Ahab's apostrophe. Thus, "Then hail for ever hail, O sea" works quite well as "Salut, donc—salut à jamais, ô mer"[5] (even if more than a little is lost rhythmically) because French has its own tradition of elevated literary language and lofty forms of address. Not surprisingly, Melville's explosive alliterations have entirely vanished in the French rendering along with all the iambic cadences. What is robustly odd in the English is regularized in the French:

[5]*Moby-Dick et Pierre ou les Ambiguïtés*, under the editorial supervision of Philippe Jaworski, with the collaboration of Marc Amfreville, Dominique Marçais, Mark Niemeyer, and Hershel Parker (Paris: Gallimard, 2006) p. 539.

"Hindoo" becomes *l'Indienne*; "wide-slaughtering" is simply *destructeur*; and "unverdured" is interpretively translated and sadly flattened as *infertile*. Melville's prose is improvisatory, exuberantly unruly in its inventiveness, and in this regard inaugurates a tradition in American style; the French smoothes all this out. Perhaps most strikingly, because there is no canonical French translation of the Bible that can be tapped as Melville taps the King James Version, the strong sense of grand biblical language used to shape a vision of the world counter to that of the Bible is entirely absent. The terrific force of "who of drowned bones has builded thy separate throne in the heart of these unverdured seas" is diluted in the unbiblical "qui t'es construit, quelque part au coeur de ces mers infertiles, un trône fait des os des noyés." A reader of this perfectly competent French version will no doubt pick up a good deal of the grandeur in Ahab's address to destructive nature and to the whale, but it is bound to be a paler experience than is offered by the original's constellation of stylistic effects, including the potent biblical background they incorporate.

There is no real contradiction in my underscoring the failure of translation to convey the stylistic complexity of the original and my expressed admiration for the 1611 English rendering of the Hebrew Bible. There are surely moments in literary history when a translation, whatever its closeness to or distance from the original it represents, becomes an achievement in its own right. For reasons that we cannot entirely explain—three that come to mind are the mining of William Tyndale's brilliant version of the Bible, the richness of English literary culture at the beginning of the seventeenth century, the peculiar and productive decision to follow the contours of the Hebrew in idiom and often in syntax—the translators convened by King James shaped an English version that introduced a new model of stylistic power to the language. What usually happens, however, in translation, as in the instance of the French rendering of *Moby-Dick*, is that a dutiful, more or less semantically faithful version of the original, employing a rather conventional set of stylistic procedures, erases a good deal of what is most compelling in the original text.

There is one aspect of style in the novel that deserves special highlighting, which is the interplay of different levels and provenances of diction, because it is particularly relevant to the effect of insets of biblical language that will be examined in the remainder of this study. Language in the novel is quite often an intricate game of high and low, for reasons that are probably best explained by the Russian theorist M. M. Bakhtin, who defines the generic distinctiveness of the novel as a collision of and dialogue among different languages in the same culture, each embodying its own values and outlook. In Lincoln's oratory, there are different elements of diction, including biblical turns of speech, but one gets the sense that they have all been integrated into a single oratorical style. In the novel, on the other hand, as Bakhtin suggests, the disparateness of the different languages is preserved as they are played against each other—"builded thy separate throne" and "unnamable imminglings" belong to different linguistic realms, and each even has its own music and its own associations.

Not much critical attention these days is devoted to levels of diction, and perhaps many critics do not even hear the nuances of difference. This inattention may in part reflect broad social changes, though one also suspects a consequence of the decline of reading. The literary deployment and recognition of levels of diction are rooted in social hierarchy: what is perceived as low or even vulgar, as educated speech, or as lofty literary language, depends, at least in origin, on class distinctions. Contemporary American society exhibits a notorious and increasing economic gap between the rich and the poor, but class differentiation is less formally marked here than it has been earlier and elsewhere. The lack of such differentiation surely helps foster some insensitivity to levels of diction among American readers. Yet a neglect of the game of high and low that has been going on in the novel for three centuries dulls the perception of style and deprives readers of one of the keen pleasures in the reading experience. Thus Fielding in *Tom Jones*, in a characteristic ploy, describes Tom's dive into the bushes with the accommodating Molly Seagrim in the most highfalutin Latinate language while, with professed reluctance, introducing the term "rutting" to identify the activity in question. The contrast between the two dictions not only is amusing but also makes a moral point: a young man's acting on an impulse of lust may be hypocritically disguised by euphemistic language, but it belongs, perhaps quite appropriately and healthily, to the realm of animal behavior.

In English, the great source of stylistic counterpoint is the two dictions deriving respectively from the Greco-Latin and the Anglo-Saxon components of the language: the former, polysyllabic, learned and sometimes even recondite, often tending to abstraction; the latter, phonetically compact, often monosyllabic, broadly associated with everyday speech, and usually concrete. The language of the King James Version falls by and large on the Anglo-Saxon side of this divide, though there are abundant elements of the Anglo-Saxon stratum of the language that have nothing to do with the King James Version. The counterpointing of the two strata has been a feature of English prose since the seventeenth century, and we have already seen one striking instance of it in one of the excerpts quoted from Melville. But it is Faulkner, clearly a kind of neo-Baroque stylist, who is the great master of this strategy of contrapuntal dictions. A spectacular example is evident in the two paragraphs that begin the Dilsey chapter in *The Sound and the Fury*. There is nothing obviously biblical in the language of the passage, though it contains one freighted, paradoxical image that has a thematically important biblical background. In any case, as I shall argue in relation to *Absalom, Absalom!*, Faulkner's writing is not biblical in texture or syntax but rather in its marshalling of keywords from the biblical lexicon, and I think three such words occur here. As readers will recall, this concluding section of *The Sound and the Fury* switches from the use of the characters' points of view employed in the three previous sections to a resplendently omniscient narrator deploying high Faulknerian language:

> The day dawned bleak and chill, a moving wall of gray light out of the northeast which, instead of dissolving into moisture, seemed to disintegrate into minute and venomous particles, like dust, that when Dilsey opened the door of the cabin and emerged, needled laterally

into her flesh, precipitating not so much a moisture as a substance partaking of the quality of thin, not quite congealed oil. She wore a stiff black straw hat perched upon her turban, and a maroon velvet cape with a border of mangy and anonymous fur above a dress of purple silk, and she stood in the door for a while with her myriad and sunken face lifted to the weather, and one gaunt hand flac-soled as the belly of a fish, then she moved the cape aside and examined the bosom of her gown.

... She had been a big woman once but now her skeleton rose, draped loosely in unpadded skin that tightened again upon a paunch almost dropsical, as though muscle and tissue had been courage and fortitude which the days or the years consumed until only the indomitable skeleton was left rising like a ruin or a landmark above the somnolent and impervious guts, and above that the collapsed face that gave the impression of the bones being outside the flesh, lifted into the driving day with an expression at once fatalistic and of a child's astonished disappointment, until she turned and entered the house again and closed the door.[6]

The passage begins with a chain of monosyllabic words of Anglo-Saxon provenance—which, in accordance with the natural rhythms of English, also constitute an iambic cadence. The counterpoint to this pattern is first asserted in the initial subordinate clause, where there is an array of Latinate terms—"dissolving," "moisture," "disintegrate," "minute and venomous particles." Faulkner,

---

[6]William Faulkner, *The Sound and the Fury* (New York: Vintage, 1990), pp. 265–66.

with a kind of stylistic relish, delights in emphatically bracketing terms that reflect the contrasting dictions: "mangy and anonymous fur," "myriad and sunken face," "a paunch almost dropsical," "somnolent and impervious guts." The strong effect of these double-barreled formulations is simultaneously to give Dilsey's presence a gritty physical concreteness—an aging black woman with a sagging face and a protuberant belly wearing a moth-eaten cape—and to imbue her figure with metaphysical complication, representing her under the aspect of eternity—the wrinkles on her face are "myriad," as much a manifestation of the multiplicity and variety of life experience as of decay; the shabbiness of the fur trim becomes, wonderfully, "anonymous" just as the guts are mysteriously "impervious"; and, most evidently, Dilsey emerges through all this energetic activity of style as an image of courage and fortitude, stubbornly continuing with the chores and trials of caring for those around her despite the body's decay and the most maddening circumstances.

It must be said that this metaphysical complication of the physical description becomes, in the second paragraph, a little disorienting, though this may well be the intended effect: one does not readily visualize the image of the bones being outside the flesh. What drives that paradoxical image is Ezekiel's vision of the dry bones revived: "And I will lay sinews upon you, and will bring flesh upon you, and cover you with skin, and put breath in you, and you shall live" (Ezekiel 37:6). Although Ezekiel's original prophecy is actually an allegory of national rebirth after the metaphorical death of exile, in its later reception it became the source text for the idea of the resurrection of the dead, and its dissemination in the popular Negro spiritual is surely relevant to Faulkner's representation of Dilsey. Her chapter is set on Easter Sunday, 1928, and at the church service she will be granted a vision of the true resurrection ("I've seed de first en de last"[p. 297]). Faulkner, of course, is transposing Christian theology into a moral and un-theological perspective on human nature: Dilsey, unlike the members of the Compson family, each dead-ended in a different way, is the one figure in the novel capable of regeneration, of bearing up under life's burdens and enduring.

The word "skeleton" does not occur in Ezekiel or in any other biblical text, but after it is put forth twice here, we get "bones," which is at the center of the passage in Ezekiel and also part of a more general idiomatic pattern in the Bible. Three monosyllabic terms that figure significantly in the Bible form a constellation here: dust, flesh, and bones. (In chapter 3, we will have occasion to trace the importance of these very terms in the thematic lexicon of *Absalom, Absalom!*) It may at first seem something of a stretch to link "dust" in the first sentence of this passage with any biblical usage. It occurs here, after all, as a simile meant to convey the concrete look and feel of the gray light and moist air of dawn on this early April morning. In the Bible, dust is sometimes a metonymy for human mortality, for man who was made from dust and is fated to return to dust. But as the metaphysical complications of the representation of Dilsey accumulate in these two paragraphs, with the theme of resurrection emerging, and as "flesh" and "bones" make an appearance, which in biblical idiom are a collocation that indicates kinship and the sheer physicality of mortal human life, "dust" at the beginning seems not only a rendering of the weirdly particulate quality of the morning light and driving mist but also an intimation of the ephemeral material substance of human existence. Dilsey, like all of us, is from dust, and to dust she will return; the integument of flesh manifested in her physical appearance begins to fall away, as it must; but the bones rising from the slack flesh invoke Ezekiel's promise that new flesh will be laid on the dry bones and they will live again.

Faulkner's prose is a limit case for the decisive presence of the King James Version in a long line of American writers. His rhythms and syntax and the spectacularly recondite vocabulary he often favors are not in the least biblical. He is far removed from the biblical rhetorical sweep of Lincoln's oratory and from the flourishes of biblical poetic style that mark some of the grander moments of Melville's narrative prose. Yet, he was a writer steeped in the 1611 rendering of Scripture, and he found in it a thematic vocabulary that met the large measure he sought in his novels for the representation of the human condition. Stylistically, these compact key-terms that he drew from the Bible were, in their very concreteness, as I shall try to show later, a ballast, like the rest of his Anglo-Saxon vocabulary, against the soaring abstractions that were also vitally important for him: dust and flesh and bone over against myriad and indomitable and fortitude.

This study is an attempt to throw light on the abiding role of the King James Version in the shaping of style in the American novel and at the same time an effort to reanimate, through this particular instance of the biblical component, the sense of the importance of style in the novel. Especially because borrowings from the King James Version are always one element among many in American prose, it is worth stressing that language itself comprises highly heterogeneous elements, and hence the constituents of style in general are themselves heterogeneous and their combinations and permutations intrinsically unpredictable. The sound and length of the words (as we have just seen in Faulkner), their syntactic ordering, the cadences in which they are arranged, the levels of diction they manifest, the antecedent texts (biblical and others) they evoke explicitly or obliquely, their deployment of figurative language—all combine in shifting patterns to put an indelible stamp on one moment after another and on the entire fictional world constituted from those moments. To revert to the question of what is lost in most translation, I would say that reading the untranslatable text is ultimately what departments of literary studies ought to be about, but in the peculiar atmosphere that has dominated the academy for several decades, the reverse has often taken place: the original has been read almost as though it might as well have been a translation. Too often, though surely not invariably, teachers of literature and their hapless students have tended to look right through style to the purported grounding of the text in one ideology or another.

As I have already noted, I am by no means proposing that the context of ideology is irrelevant to the study of literature. Literary works are made of words, but they emerge from and address issues in the real world, and so politics, social history, biography, material culture, technology, and intellectual history are all worthy of attention in the effort to attain a fuller understanding of literature. What I would like to argue is that none of these considerations of context should entail an averted gaze from the artful, inventive, and often startlingly original use of language that is the primary stuff of literature, the very medium through which it takes in history, politics, society, and everything else. The play of style in fiction is not only a source of deep pleasure, sometimes even rapture, but also a process that enables thought, inviting the perception of complex associative links, compelling fine discriminations and qualifications, leading us to see one frame of meaning in connection with another, or with several others. The King James Version of the Bible, once justifiably thought of as the national book of the American people, helped foster, at least for two centuries, a general responsiveness to the expressive, dignified use of language, to the ways in which the rhythms and diction of a certain kind of English could move readers. Against this general background, I would now like to explore some eminent instances in which novelists drew on the resources of the King James Version to fashion different versions of a distinctive American style for prose fiction.

Chapter 2

ॐ

Moby-Dick
Polyphony

*N*othing like the prose of *Moby-Dick* had been seen before in American fiction, which is one reason why it would take well over half a century for Melville's masterpiece to receive the general appreciation it deserved. Indeed, very little like the prose of *Moby-Dick* is visible in the first four novels Melville published in quick succession before 1851—novels in which the writing can be quite vivid but is also a little hampered by that self-conscious, slightly stiff literariness often detectible in American prose of the antebellum era. The astonishing stylistic achievement of *Moby-Dick* is intimately bound up with Melville's vast ambition to make this book an American epic, an American tragedy, an American encyclopedia, and an American bible all at once. For all these aims, he found rich stylistic veins to mine in the English literature of the seventeenth century. As scholarship has often observed, the period when he was gestating *Moby-Dick* was when he seriously discovered Shakespeare, and *Lear* in particular would play a crucial role in the poetic language of his novel. *Paradise Lost*, as we are alerted by the epigraph drawn from it on the title page, was another model (Melville's copy was heavily marked in the margins), a work in blank verse like Shakespeare's plays, though employing a rather different poetic register. From Sir Thomas Browne, who is cited among the Extracts at the beginning of the novel, Melville may have learned something about the counterpointing of Anglo-Saxon and Greco-Latin terms that is one of the great stylistic resources of the English language. And, of course, this extraordinarily fertile moment in English literature nearly four centuries ago also saw the publication of the King James Version of the Bible, a translation exhibiting some kinship in diction to contemporaneous texts though, as we have noted, it was a little archaic even at the time, whether because of the translators' consciousness that they were representing an ancient and sacred language or because they were freely borrowing from the great Tyndale translation that preceded them by nearly a century.

There is an unfettered exuberance of invention and improvisation in the line of American prose that I shall be following which has no real British counterpart. Dickens, whom I would rate as the greatest stylist among British novelists in the nineteenth century, has his own linguistic exuberance, which frequently produces the most fantastic and beguiling inventions of metaphor, but on the whole it is played out within the decorum of an accepted order of literary language. The American stylistic turn that begins with Melville is to violate linguistic decorums with the greatest gusto. The general impulse is to fashion a language for the novel out of the most violently heterogeneous elements. The Bible, then, is a strong thread in the prose of *Moby-Dick* that is freely intertwined with Shakespeare, Milton, the English Baroque prose writers of the seventeenth century, sailors' argot (or a literary stylization of it), and the colloquial Yankee speech of antebellum New England. Melville's novel lies well beyond the range of texts considered by M. M. Bakhtin, but the Russian theorist's notion of heteroglossia, where in the frame of novels languages from different sectors of society (and in Melville also from different eras), encoding different values, collide, interact, and interfuse, is vigorously displayed in *Moby-Dick*. Melville makes us explicitly conscious of this energetic joining of disparate languages early in the book. When Queequeg is sworn in as a crew member by Captain Bildad, the old Quaker ship-owner addresses the imposing Pacific islander in the following vivid words: "if thou still clingest to thy Pagan ways, which I sadly fear, I beseech thee, remain not for aye a Belial bondsman. Spurn the idol Bel, and the hideous dragon; turn from the wrath to come; mind thine eye, I say; oh! goodness gracious! steer clear of the fiery pit!"[1] Now, Bildad is a Bible-reading Quaker—he has been studying Scripture, his partner Peleg reminds him, more than thirty years, with no sign of finishing—and so it is not surprising that his language should be suffused with biblicisms: lexical items such as "cling," "beseech," "bondsman," "spurn," "wrath," and explicit allusions to Belial, Bel the dragon, and the fiery pit. What should also be noted, for

[1] Herman Melville, *Moby-Dick*, edited by Harrison Heyford and Hershel Parker (New York: W.W. Norton, 1967), p. 85.

we shall be encountering other instances of this pattern,
is that Bildad's speech takes the form of semantic parallelism that is the fundamental organizing principle of
biblical poetry. (His namesake in the Book of Job, one
of Job's three adversarial friends, is someone who actually speaks biblical poetry.) The fact that Bildad is a
Quaker provides realistic motivation for his use of the
old "thou" and "thee," which are equally biblical. The
locution "for aye" and the slightly puzzling "mind thine
eye" are archaic but not specifically biblical. To all these
is added the euphemistic expletive "goodness gracious,"
which is genteel American colloquial.

Despite the strong predominance of biblical elements
in this speech of Bildad's, it is its heterogeneity that Melville's narrator chooses to emphasize in commenting on
it: "Something of the old salt sea yet lingered in old
Bildad's language, heterogeneously mixed with Scriptural and domestic phrases." In fact, there is nothing
evident of the old salt sea in this bit of dialogue, though
of course it is abundantly present elsewhere in the nautical speech of the novel, as when Ahab passes round
the pewter mug of grog in the ceremony dedicating the
harpooners: "Short draughts—long swallows, men; 'tis
hot as Satan's hoof.... It spiralizes in ye; forks out at the
serpent-snapping eye" (p. 145). One should observe that
though the references to Satan and the serpent are biblical, the colloquial language, with its explosive al+litera-
tions ("hot as Satan's hoof," "the serpent-snapping eye"),
is not. And then, in consonance with Melville's commitment to the orchestration of linguistic heterogeneity,
there is the wonderful invention of "it spiralizes in ye," a
locution neither nautical nor biblical featuring a vividly

concocted verb that exists in English only here, for the nonce.

What Ishmael notes about Bildad's spoken language is generally true of his own language as narrator. "His own," to be sure, is a somewhat problematic term because Ishmael famously, or notoriously, disappears as an individualized character presenting a first-person narration into an authoritative, often poetic narrator who is the author's mouthpiece. In any case, since neither Ishmael nor Melville's poetic persona is a Scripture-quoting Quaker, the biblical elements, important as they may be, are on the whole far less dominant than they are in Bildad's speech. But the athletic leapfrogging from biblicisms to high Shakespearian and Miltonic blank verse (the prose often assuming iambic cadences) to American colloquial and sailors' speech gives Ishmael's narrative an expressive elasticity and an evocative power that are new in the American novel.

In many instances, these disparate stylistic materials are placed together contrapuntally, producing nice effects of contrast. Since syntax is the skeletal structure of language, it may be useful to observe this process first on the level of syntax. The haunting moment when the *Pequod* sets sail on a cold Christmas afternoon is initially registered in a little sequence of subordinate clauses: " . . . as the short northern day merged into night, we found ourselves almost broad upon the wintry ocean, whose freezing spray cased us in ice, as in polished armor" (p. 95). The striking image of the polished armor then metamorphoses into a much more fantastic simile in the next sentence: "the long rows of teeth on the bulwarks glistened in the moonlight, and like the white ivory tusks of some huge elephant, vast curving icicles depended from the bows." This is a sentence that could conceivably have been written by Dickens, whose figurative language very often exhibits such leaps of fantasy, and who often favors such elegant formality (in fact he is fond of this use of "depend" in its literal Latin sense of "hang down").

The very next sentence, however, which begins a new paragraph, switches syntactic gears, and with that switch, there is also a detectible shift in diction:

> Lank Bildad, as pilot, headed the first watch, and ever and anon, as the old craft dived deep in the green seas, and sent the shivering frost all over her, and the winds howled, and the cordage rang, his steady notes were heard,—
>
> > "Sweet fields beyond the swelling flood,
> > Stand dressed in living green.
> > So to the Jews old Canaan stood,
> > While Jordan rolled between."

There is a weird and wrenching irony in Bildad's chanting this Christian hymn, which evokes a pastoral vision of the Promised Land, as the *Pequod* sets sail into the yawning maw of chaos. But I suspect that the biblical landscape of the hymn triggers a preparatory biblicizing turn in the structure of the sentence that precedes it. Parataxis, the form of syntax that strings together parallel units joined by the connective "and," governs the sentence. This is not a kind of syntax that is at home in early modern or modern English, or, at any rate, it was not at home until the appearance of the King James Version, which generally, though not invariably, follows the syntactic pattern of the Hebrew. Here, for example, is Rebekah at the well in the 1611 English version: "and she hasted, and emptied her pitcher into the trough, and ran again unto the well to draw *water*, and drew for all his camels" (Genesis 24:20). Or Esau completing the transaction of the sale of his birthright: "Then Jacob gave Esau bread and pottage of lentils; and he did eat and drink, and rose up, and went his way: thus Esau despised *his* birthright" (Genesis 26:34). (The Hebrew for this verse is even more unswervingly paratactic than the King James Version: Both "then" at the beginning of the first clause and "thus" at the beginning of the last are actually "and" [the connective particle *vav* in the Hebrew]). Concomitant with the parataxis is a move away from the more traditional literary diction of the preceding sentences, which naturally accommodates such polysyllabic terms as "depended," "elephant," and "icicles," to a language in which monosyllabic words, for the most part of Anglo-Saxon derivation, predominate. This is, by and large, the diction favored by the King James translators, though one word here, "howled," is not noticeably biblical but does play a significant role in *King Lear*, as it will in *Moby-Dick*. There is a cleanness of line in the simplicity of the diction, driving forward relentlessly in the paratactic chain as the ice-encased whaler itself cuts forward through the cold waters toward the open sea, that makes a strong stylistic counterpoint to the whole previous paragraph. Both the diction and the syntax, with their biblical background, will attract, as we shall see, a number of later American novelists, from Hemingway and Gertrude Stein to Cormac McCarthy.

   In the Hebrew Bible, the correlative to parataxis in
the narrative prose is parallelism in the poetry. Semantic
parallelism has been understood as the organizing formal principle of biblical poetry since the lectures of
Bishop Lowth on this subject in the eighteenth century.
It scarcely matters whether Melville was consciously
aware of the principle because, manifestly, in his reading
and rereading of the King James Version, these patterns
were deeply incised in his memory as a prose-poet (and
the border between poetry and prose would surely have
been conveniently blurred for him by the fact that the
King James Version offers no typographic indication of
lines of verse for the poetry). I will quote just one illustrative instance of the biblical poetic system from Job,
the biblical book that is most important for *Moby-Dick*:
"Why did I not die from the womb? *why* did I *not* give
up the ghost when I came out of the belly? Why did the
knees prevent me? or why the breasts that I should
suck?" (Job 3:11–12). These two verses correspond to
two lines of Hebrew poetry. Each line, in turn, comprises two parallel utterances marked by semantically
matching terms: "died"/"give up the ghost," "womb"/
"belly," "knees"/"breasts." It is also worth observing,
because I think Melville picked this up subliminally,
that there is a certain narrative momentum in the parallelism: from the image of being stillborn in the womb
the poet moves to coming out of the belly to die and then
in the next line to the birth of the infant, "prevented"
(that is, anticipated or greeted) by the mother's knees
and then sucking at her breasts. The English version, at
one point indulging in an extravagant proliferation of
words ("*why* did I *not* give up the ghost when I came out

of the belly," a half-line that in the Hebrew is three compact words, three stresses, *mibéten yats'áti ve'egvá'*),
somewhat obscures the poetic rhythm of the Hebrew.
This masking of the formal rhythm, however, would
have encouraged Melville as an English reader to see the
biblical poetry as a loose form of elevated discourse
straddling poetry and prose and hence eminently suited
to his own purposes. What he clearly must have registered is the structure of parallelism.

That structure is by no means pervasive in the prose
of *Moby-Dick*, but intermittently recurring through the
book, it does add a distinctive coloration to the language
of this novel. At the end of the first chapter, as Ishmael
reports being tormented by "an everlasting itch for
things remote," he observes, "I love to sail forbidden
seas, and land on barbarous coasts." This sentence, with
its two semantically parallel clauses that also inscribe a
narrative progression from sailing to landing, could easily be a line of biblical poetry. The link with poetry is
reinforced by the rhythm, a four-beat, three-beat iambic
cadence. The next sentence begins with a looser form of
parallelism, employing the complementary antithetical
pairing one finds in many lines of biblical poetry (as in
"Let the day perish... , and the night" in the very first
line of verse spoken by Job): "Not ignoring what is good,
I am quick to perceive a horror." At this juncture, in
consonance with Melville's cultivation of a vigorous ad-
mixture of styles, Ishmael abandons parallelism altogether as he switches to Yankee-colloquial tinged with
jocularity: "and could still be social with it—would they
let me—since it is but well to be on friendly terms with
all the inmates of the place one lodges in" (p. 16).

In any case, interesting variations on the poetic parallelism of the Bible continue to surface in *Moby-Dick*.
Reflecting on the blind lethal power of the sea, Melville's
narrator comments: "But not only is the sea such a foe
to man who is an alien to it, but also a fiend to its own
offspring; worse than the Persian host who murdered his
own guests; sparing not the creatures which itself hath
spawned" (p. 235). The two long clauses here, divided
by a semicolon, each with two semantically parallel constituents, could almost read as two lines of biblical poetry. In fact the word pair "enemies"/"foes" or "enemies"/
"adversaries" is quite common in biblical poetry, especially
in Psalms (Melville no doubt opted for "fiend" in its
older sense of "enemy" because of the alliterative and
rhythmic matching with "foe"). The second long clause
also picks up another feature of biblical parallelism,
which is its pronounced tendency to intensify or heighten
an idea introduced in the first half of the line in the second: first the sea murders its human guests and, then, in
the parallel utterance, it destroys the very creatures it
has begotten.

At times, biblical parallelism produces compressed
but strong shocking effects in the prose. Here is a brief
sentence conveying the wracking somatic anguish imposed on Ahab by his vengeful obsession with the white
whale: "He sleeps with clenched hands; and wakes with
his own bloody nails" (p. 174). Biblical scholars would
probably call this complementary parallelism, but something more interesting than complementarity is going
on. There is a focusing intensification from the first clause
to the second, from clenched hands to bloody nails, and
also a narrative progression from the clenching of the

hands at the beginning of the night to the self-wounding that is visible upon waking. The gap or ellipsis between the first utterance and the second, which generates a certain power by enlisting the reader to fill it in, is equally characteristic of poetry and prose in the Bible. In all this, I think Melville shows himself to be not only a writer who keenly observed biblical themes and images and explicitly incorporated them in his fiction but also a stylist who deeply assimilated some of the Bible's distinctive modes of expression.

My last brief example of biblical poetic parallelism in Melville's prose is also a vigorous instance of his mixture of styles. In the chapter entitled "The Try-Works," in which the rendering of the whale's blubber is elaborately described, Ishmael says of the odor that the procedure produces, "It smells like the left wing of the day of judgment; it is an argument for the pit" (p. 353). Again, one could say that the sentence, employing two coordinate clauses separated by a semicolon, readily "scans" as a line of parallelistic verse. "Day of judgment" and its matching term, "the pit," are eminently biblical locutions. The phrase "it is an argument for" belongs to a distinctly unbiblical realm of discourse, either lawyerly or philosophical, with perhaps a Yankee intonation; and "the left wing" attached to "the day of judgment" sounds altogether colloquial. In 1851, it could not yet have been a football term, but it is an inspired ad hoc invention, drawing on the idea that the left is the bad side and perhaps on the notion that both angels and demons have wings, and invoking the pungent spoken American language in the midst of biblicisms.

Style obviously cannot be separated from narrative

stance or from theme. I have used the rather general phrase "narrative stance" rather than a technical narratological term because much of what goes on in *Moby-Dick* is not through what is conventionally called narrative point of view but through a variety of rhetorical interpellations of the reader by the narrator. The predominant maneuver is homiletic. With the Bible and the American church tradition of expounding the Bible so constantly in the novelist's mind, it is hardly surprising that many of the discourses Melville introduces in the novel should take the form of homilies. The most spectacular instance, of course, is Father Mapple's sermon on the Book of Jonah, in which the subject is biblical through and through while the vividness of the sermon derives from its being so brilliantly cast in the language of "the old salt sea." But again and again in the novel we encounter compact homilies in which the narrator invites us to contemplate the symbolic or explicitly allegorical meaning of a given subject as a "sign and symbol" (a phrase Melville uses more than once) of the human condition in the vast and indifferent cosmos. These are manifestly subversive, un-Christian homilies, even as they invoke the allegorical strategies of Christian tradition and the terms of sacred Scripture. Here is a characteristic instance, the concluding paragraph of chapter 58 on the murderous sea, a chapter from which I have already quoted:

> Consider all this; and then turn to this green, gentle, and most docile earth; consider them both, the sea and the land; and do you not find a strange analogy to something in yourself? For as this appalling ocean surrounds

the verdant land, so in the soul there lies one insular
Tahiti, full of peace and joy, but encompassed by all the
horrors of the half known life. God keep thee! Push not
off from that isle, thou canst never return! (p. 236)

The narrator's homiletic stance is explicitly signaled
at the beginning by the doubled "consider this," "consider then," and by the underscoring of the reference to
"a strange analogy to something in yourself." The language is sermonic rather than biblical, with the Christian notion of "peace and joy" gravely compromised by
its being a mere interior island, "one insular Tahiti,"
surrounded by an ocean of horrors beyond human ken.
(This idea is reinforced by the color symbolism: the
ocean is "appalling," that is, makes one turn pale, a reiterated word in *Moby-Dick* associated with the white-
ness of the whale, and the verdant island within is but a
dream of paridisal refuge.) The little homily concludes,
however, by switching to biblical diction, a shift marked
by the move from the modern "you" in the first sentence
to the archaic "thee" and "thou" at the end. "God keep
thee!" is nearly a quotation from the threefold priestly
blessing in Leviticus. The final sentence with its two balanced clauses, "Push not off from that isle, thou canst
never return!," approaches the structure of parallelism
of a line of biblical poetry. It is not quite an allusion, but
it corresponds in formulation to the warning about the
daunting power of the Leviathan, "Lay thine hand upon
him, remember the battle, do no more" (Job 41:8), and
is even closer to the evocation in Proverbs 2:19 of the
seductress as a treacherous bottomless pit, "None that

go unto her return again, neither take they hold of the paths of life."

If here any specific biblical text is no more than an oblique recollection, elsewhere, as the language glides into biblical diction, a remembered text from Scripture is polemically and exegetically engaged. (In this and in other respects, Melville directs his attention not only to the Bible proper but also to the body of Christian interpretation of the Bible, often proposing subversive readings that run against the grain of the accepted ones.) Thus, at the end of a chapter devoted to a disquisition on the tail of the whale (chapter 86), which is conducted in expository-encyclopedic prose (still another style deployed in this novel), the narrator again switches diction.

> But if I know not even the tail of the whale, how understand his head? much more, how comprehend his face, when face he has none? Thou shalt see my back parts, my tail, he seems to say, but my face shall not be seen. But I cannot completely make out his back parts; and hint what he will about his face, I say again he has no face. (p. 318)

The change in style is already reflected in the syntactic inversion of "I know not," which yields a more compact rhythm than the normal prosaic word order ("I do not know"). The entire first sentence, exhibiting an a fortiori structure, reads like a triadic line of biblical poetry ("if I know not," "how understood," "much more, how comprehend"), with the subordinate clause at the end, "when face he has none," superadded, yet preserving in its syntactic inversion the archaic poetic formality of the whole. In the body of the chapter the narrator uses "you" for the second-person singular. Here, once again, as the language becomes biblical, he switches to "thou" in the midst of the most audacious allusion to Scripture: "Thou shalt see my back parts... but my face shall not be seen." Melville is pointedly invoking God's words to Moses on Mount Sinai, "Thou canst not see my face: for there shall no man see me and live.... thou shalt see my back parts: but my face shall not be seen" (Exodus 33:20, 23). We should not fall into the trap, as some commentators on this novel have done, of concluding that Melville hereby equates the whale with God. What the arresting allusion does suggest is that there is a correspondence between the ancient Hebrew God, unapproachable, unrepresentable, overwhelming, and the looming creature that in the novel is the chief avatar of the inscrutability and the blind power of the natural world. In this as in many other ways, we would do well to think of Melville as a post-theistic writer. That is to say, he comes after a highly charged theistic tradition, and though he no longer believes in the personal and providential God of Christian faith, he manifestly still carries the weight of theistic ideas, struggling with it, imagining a more savage god, or sometimes none at all.

At this point, then, the biblical diction enables a bold heterodox engagement with a particularly fraught biblical text. Finally, the concluding sentence here registers still another shift in diction: "But I cannot completely make out his back parts; and hint what he will about his face, I say again he has no face." The poetic cadences of the preceding sentences relax into a language that sounds much more like spoken English, especially evident in the colloquial turn of "I cannot completely make out." The speaker we hear at the end is a plausible nineteenth-century American, perhaps actually the Ishmael with whom the novel began, pondering the daunting impenetrability of what he has just evoked and emphatically announcing, "I say again he has no face." One might describe this whole chapter as a microscopic instance of Melvillian heteroglossia, though I'm not sure whether the relationship of the three languages—encyclopedic, biblical, and colloquial—is dialogic according to the terms of Bakhtin's influential theory. Perhaps it might be better to apply an allied concept Bakhtin used in his earlier work, polyphony. That is, there may be no real difference in underlying values or ideology among Melville's different languages, but he does seem to be reaching for an orchestration of aesthetic effect in creating this compendious American novel in which many voices are resonantly joined together. The language of the British novel—Fielding, Jane Austen, Walter Scott—had by and large been unitary, and that is a model which Melville zestfully breaks apart. Perhaps only Joyce would be more extreme in the proliferation of languages in a single novel, and, of course, Joyce was not British either.

If Melville's stylistic polyphony is not predominantly the vehicle for a dialogue of different viewpoints, it does make possible a complex interplay of tones. The tonality of the prose of *Moby-Dick* is one of its most peculiar features, and not easy to keep in focus in discussing the novel. One readily recalls the many high-poetic passages that above all sound like Shakespeare—most memorably, those riveting descriptions of the whaling boats tossed like helpless chips in the churning wake of their prey, descriptions that tap the language used in *Lear* on the moor battered by the storm. Such moments are obviously counterpointed by the sections of dry expository writing devoted to the details of the whaling industry, but they are also set off by the recurrent slides into jocularity, often accompanied by dips into colloquial diction. It is a bizarre kind of jocularity, frequently used to express rather grim thoughts. It is as though Melville, exploiting the formal fluidity of the novel, wanted to have the grotesque comedy of the gatekeeper in *Macbeth* and the "tomorrow and tomorrow" soliloquy all in one breath.

At one point, for example, the narrator finds himself wondering "whether Leviathan can long endure so wide a chase, and so remorseless a havoc; whether he must not at last be exterminated from the waters, and the last whale, like the last man, smoke his last pipe, and then evaporate in the final puff" (p. 383). The weird comparison between man and whale is no doubt motivated by the visual analogy between the spouting of the whale and the smoke going up from a pipe. The way Melville refers to the fantastic image of the last man evaporating in the final puff from his own pipe suggests that he may be drawing on a current joke. Yet the subject is no joking matter. Ishmael is contemplating the extinction of the species that he has been representing as the very crown of creation. By linking the extinction of the whale with the disappearance of the last man, he gives the idea apocalyptic implications. Through a jocular gesture we arrive at the preeminently biblical notion of apocalypse, though nothing in the language here is biblical. The edgy jocular fantastication, one might add, is another feature of style that reflects an affinity with Dickens.

An odd jocular note sometimes even creeps into those passages that I have characterized as secular homilies. I would like to quote one of these at length because, as it explicitly invokes two Old Testament books, it articulates the nature of Melville's heterodox engagement with the Bible, which in the end is more instructive than simply identifying his biblical allusions. I shall pick up the passage at the point where the homiletic gesture is emphatically stressed: "The sun hides not the ocean, which is the dark side of the earth. So, therefore, that mortal man who hath more of joy than sorrow in him, that mortal man cannot be true—not true, or undeveloped. With books the same." The language of didactic analogy ("The sun hides...," "So, therefore...") announces the lesson to be presented. More than once in the novel the narrator muses over the topographical fact that more than two thirds of the terrestrial globe is covered by the ocean, a realm of chaos and destruction predominating over the illusory sphere of order of dry land. *Moby-Dick* is set on the high seas in order to be "true" to the appalling nature of the reality we inhabit. The homilist continues:

> The truest of all men was the Man of Sorrows, and the truest of all books is Solomon's, and Ecclesiastes is the fine hammered steel of woe. "All is vanity." ALL. This wilful world hath not got hold of un-Christian Solomon's wisdom yet. But he who dodges hospitals and jails, and walks fast crossing grave-yards, and would rather talk of operas than hell; calls Cowper, Young, Pascal, Rousseau poor devils all of sick men; and throughout a care-free lifetime swears by Rabelais as passing wise, and therefore jolly;—not that man is fitted to sit down

on tomb-stones, and break the green damp mould with unfathomably wondrous Solomon. (p. 355)

Christ is mentioned in a passing gesture, chiefly for his epithet, the Man of Sorrows, which suits the rhetorical purpose of the homily. Melville does not, however, want to linger on the Man of Sorrows, nor does he invoke the Gospels as texts, because the essential idea of Christ's redeeming love of mankind, the very reason He becomes the Man of Sorrows, is antithetical to the truth about the world that Melville means to convey. The author—at least as he is represented by tradition—of Ecclesiastes and Proverbs is identified as "un-Christian Solomon" for the obvious reason that he lived a thousand years before the Christian dispensation. But I think that Melville saw him as un-Christian in a profounder sense. The traditional Christian reader, viewing Hebrew Scripture through the lens of typology, is primed to see everywhere in it adumbrations of Christian ideas and theology. Melville, on the other hand, evinces a firm sense that there are parts of the Hebrew Bible that vehemently dissent from the mainline version of biblical monotheism on which Christianity was built. It is precisely for this reason that Job is so important for him— not merely because it spectacularly features Leviathan in the great poem from the Whirlwind but because its Leviathan and the whole revelation from the Whirlwind manifest a dazzling, powerful, and sometimes cruel creation over which man, in contradiction to Genesis, has no control and which is beyond his ken. Ecclesiastes, with its bleak, unblinking vision of endless cycles of futility, is another dissenting text, questioning not divine justice and man's place in creation but the possibility of enduring value and meaningful human action. One should note how Melville's prose catches fire when he mentions this book: "Ecclesiastes is the fine hammered steel of woe." In a characteristic switch of registers, this poetic moment, marked by strong figurative language, is followed by the colloquial turn of "not got hold of" and the man "who dodges hospitals and jails." Melville then offers a little roll call of writers—none of whom in the least resembles him—associated with somber or downright gloomy themes, while the exuberant Rabelais is offered as an obvious antithesis. It is an inadvertent irony that, stylistically, Rabelais, with his riot of languages and his improvisatory zest, is a good deal closer to Melville than any of the purported purveyors of gloom listed here. The peculiar final gesture of this paragraph is another instance of Melville's propensity to introduce jocular half-notes into dark meditations. The person who skirts around the ineluctable reality of death and despair is unsuited "to sit down on tomb-stones, and break the green damp mould with unfathomable wondrous Solomon." This is, I think, a kind of macabre joke. Solomon was the wisest of men, not for the legendary reason given in the Book of Kings, but because he wrote Ecclesiastes and the gloomier verses of the Book of Proverbs. Spiritual conviviality with wondrous Solomon would be a meeting in a graveyard, where instead of breaking bread together with him one would break green damp mould. Melville through Ishmael here expresses a deep sense of kinship with one of the dissenting writers of the Hebrew Bible (Christian Scripture does not offer him similar resources), and in the sentence immediately following the passage I have excerpted, he actually quotes a verse from Proverbs, giving it an odd exegetical spin in order to make it accord with his own grim homily. But in this instance the compelling engagement in Scripture is not accompanied by the introduction of scriptural elements in the language.

Let me cite a final instance of the Melvillian homily in which a subtle thread of biblical expression defines the pattern of significance of the interweave of languages. It also happens to be an instance of Melville's freedom from the racism of his era,[2] for it is a paean to Pip, the black cabin boy who will die by drowning.

> They were nearly all Islanders in the Pequod, *Isola-toes* too, I call such, not acknowledging the common continent of men, but each *Isolato* living on a separate continent of his own. Yet now, federated along one keel, what a set these Isolatoes were! An Anacharsis Clootz deputation from all the isles of the sea, and all the ends of the earth, accompanying Old Ahab in the Pequod to lay the world's grievances before that bar from which not very many of them ever came back. Black Little Pip—he never did! Poor Alabama boy! On the grim Pequod's forecastle ye shall ere long see him, beating his tambourine; prelusive of the eternal time, when sent for, to the great quarter-deck on high, he was bid strike in with the angels, and beat his tambourine in glory; called a coward here, hailed a hero there. (p. 108)

Turning the idea of being an islander into an allegory of the human condition by way of the Spanish cognate, *iso-*

---

[2]On Melville's opposition to racism, see Andrew Delbanco, *Melville: His World and Work* (New York: Knopf, 2005), pp. 156–58.

lato, is a preeminently homiletic device (and might even be a rejoinder to "No man is an island entire of itself" from the most famous of Donne's *Devotions Upon Emergent Occasions*). Ishmael's diction in the homily has strong colloquial elements ("I call such," "what a set these Isolatoes were") laced with nautical references ("the great quarter-deck on high") and thus has a certain kinship with the language of Father Mapple's sermon. At the point just before the end when Pip with his tambourine is set against the backdrop of eternity, there is a momentary heightening of diction in "prelusive of eternal time," that unusual adjective, surely an inkhorn term (and first recorded by the Oxford English Dictionary in a 1605 text) reminiscent of the English Baroque writers and introduced here to impart a sense of grandeur to Pip's musical performance in the masque of eternity. Nothing in the passage qualifies as an actual citation of Scripture, but immediately after the metaphorical reference to Anacharsis Clootz's motley deputation at the French National Assembly of 1790, we encounter "from all the isles of the sea, and all the ends of the earth." These paired phrases not only make a nice biblical poetic parallelism, but both "the isles of the sea" and "the ends of the earth" are recurrent biblical locutions, the former a set idiom for distant places and the latter a poetic formula for the whole wide world, all of existence that we can imagine. The phrases look innocent enough because "sea" and "earth" are rather ordinary English terms, but their biblical background imbues Ishmael's characterization of the *Pequod*'s crew with a nuance of poetic dignity and cosmic grandeur, in the midst of his nautical-colloquial language. The striking image of laying "all the world's grievances before that bar" from which few return may not sound biblical, but it is ultimately inspired by Job's repeated insistence that he would like to have his day in court to argue his case against God.

Biblical cadence reappears at the end of the homily, though without any reminiscence of biblical terms, making a strong formal closure: "he was bid strike in with angels, / and beat his tambourine in glory; // called a coward here, / hailed a hero there." These clauses read like two lines of biblical poetry (I have indicated the break between the half-lines with a slash). The poetic parallelism of the second pair of phrases is especially pronounced because the rhythmic sequence of each of the half-lines is identical (stressed-unstressed-stressed-unstressed-stressed), and each half is defined by an alliteration (*c*alled a *c*oward, *h*ailed a *h*ero), the result being a perfect antithetical parallelism, a device frequently used in biblical poetry. In much of *Moby-Dick* Melville manifestly seeks to create an aura of epic prestige for his seafaring plebian characters. His decisive poetic models were Shakespeare and Milton (more the former than the latter), but he also had an intimate familiarity with Job, the Psalms, the Prophets, and the rest of biblical poetry to the extent of unconsciously internalizing some of the basic patterns of expression of the ancient Hebrew poets; and these, too, became a stylistic resource for him.

This ambition to turn the language of the novel into prose-poetry is a distinctively American project; there is nothing quite like it in British fiction till the advent of modernism. In saying this, and, indeed, in my general account of the presence of the King James Version in American prose, I do not mean to make any larger claim about the much debated issue of American exceptionalism. There are certainly some characteristic traits of American culture that look distinctive, but they do not necessarily encompass the culture as a whole and they are not necessarily unique. It suffices for my argument that the phenomena I describe are particularly at home in the American setting and are not readily imaginable elsewhere. In regard to the bold polyphony of Melville's prose that is inseparable from its purposefully poetic character, it should be stressed that there is considerable correspondence between the actual allusions to earlier writers and components of style drawn from them. The central figure of Ahab is a compound of literary allusions. He resembles King Ahab not only as evil monarch but in his heroic defiance: King Ahab at the end, bleeding to death, asks to be propped up in his chariot so that he can continue to do battle, just as Melville's Ahab at the end, blinded, his boat splintered, persists in the fierce struggle against his terrible foe ("from hell's heart I stab at thee"). Ahab is also Job, bitterly arguing against what he sees as the skewed moral order of creation, and he is even the blighted generation of the Hebrew people wandering forty years in the wilderness ("forty years of continual whaling! forty years of privation, and peril, and storm-time! forty years on the pitiless sea!" [p. 443]).[3]

[3]The standard critical work on Melville's biblical allusions for many decades has been Nathalia Wright, *Melville's Use of the Bible* (New York: Farrar, Straus and Giroux [second edition], 1980), which is scrupulous if a little mechanical. A much subtler and more perceptive treatment of the subject, stressing Melville's complex hermeneutic relationship with the Bible

At the same time, Ahab is also Milton's Satan and both Macbeth and Lear. What needs to be kept in mind is that Melville summons up for his own novelistic purposes not only the lineaments of these sundry figures but elements of the poetic language in which they are etched in the texts where they originally appear. The poetry, of course, is most memorable in the scenes on the open sea in which daring man, in all the stubborn presumption of his human courage, confronts the primordial beast he has made his prey. I shall quote just one such moment out of many. Three boats have set out from the *Pequod* in pursuit of a whale, and, a harpoon having penetrated deep into the creature (it is not Moby-Dick), it dives below the surface, hauling the harpoon's long rope down after it. The three boats, scarcely moving, wait tensely for the whale to surface from the invisible depths into the brightness of the tropical sun that beats down on them:

> As the three boats lay there on that gently rolling sea, gazing down into its eternal blue noon; and not a single groan or cry of any sort, nay, not so much as a ripple or a bubble came up from its depths; what landsman would have thought, that beneath all that silence and placidity, the utmost monster of the sea was writhing and wrenching in agony! Not eight inches of perpendicular rope were visible at the bows. Seems it credible that by three such thin threads the great Leviathan was suspended like the big weight to an eight day clock. Suspended?

---

and his penchant for associating a single figure with several biblical models, is Ilana Pardes, *Melville's Bibles* (Berkeley: University of California Press, 2008).

and to what? To three bits of board. Is this the creature of whom it was once so triumphantly said—"Canst thou fill his skin with barbed irons? or his head with fish-spears? The sword of him that layeth at him cannot hold, the spear, the dart nor the habergeon; he esteemeth iron as straw; the arrow cannot make him flee; darts are counted as stubble; he laugheth at the shaking of a spear!" This the creature? this he? Oh! that unfulfilments should follow the prophets. For with the strength of a thousand thighs in his tail, Leviathan has run his head under the mountains of the sea to hide him from the Pequod's fish-spears! (p. 300)

This is a breathtaking moment, evoked with great delicacy and deploying a variety of stylistic resources. The passage begins in quietly poised poetic diction, with no obvious allusive traits, that seems beautifully adequate to the subject of anxious expectation—"gazing down into its eternal blue noon," "not so much as a ripple or a bubble came up from its depths." The perceived stillness of the whale down below will be brilliantly complemented in the next paragraph when the narrator, having described the long late afternoon shadows cast by the boats into the water, will wonder how it all looks from the viewpoint of the whale below: "Who can tell how appalling to the wounded whale must have been such huge phantoms flitting over his head!" (The rhetorical question has an affinity with the series of rhetorical questions that God poses at the beginning of the speech from the Whirlwind.) "The utmost monster of the sea" is a little epic flourish vaguely reminiscent of Milton, whereas the strong alliteration and the palpable physicality of "writhing and wrenching" is pure Melville. Then we get an arresting small shift in register: "Not eight inches of perpendicular rope were visible at the bows." This is the eye and the language of a carpenter or a builder, gauging things with steady precision, and so adding a touch of sharply concrete definition to the scene after the epic gesture that precedes it. A still more striking instance of this contrapuntal strategy is evident in the next sentence: "Seems it credible that by three such thin threads the great Leviathan was suspended like the big weight to an eight day clock." The great Leviathan, as Melville is keenly aware, is not just a fancy synonym for the whale but a looming creature from the world of myth. Yet a mere three thin threads—the entwined strands of the rope—hold him hanging "like the big weight to an eight day clock": in a sudden vernacular turn, the utmost monster of the deep is tied in to the familiar realm of nineteenth-century domestic technology, likened to a piece from an inert thing wholly fashioned by human hands for human use. This contradiction is then driven home in the terse sentence—five words, five compact syllables—that reduces the boats in a hyperbolic synecdoche "To three bits of board."

It is at this point that the narrator quotes five full verses from the speech from the Whirlwind (Job 41:7, 26–29). We have seen how biblical references and biblical language abound in the novel, but such extensive citation is untypical, and it is worth pondering why Melville has chosen to do it here. He is, to begin with, attracted by the sheer power of the biblical poem, evoking so wonderfully the great Leviathan's impregnability in the face of all the weapons puny man can muster. The citation from Job sharply cuts two ways. On the one hand, it exposes, as the sentences immediately after the quotation spell out, the gap between Scripture and observed reality, the scandal of the "unfulfilments" of biblical prophecy. This is a tack Melville often takes in relation to the Bible: Holy Writ promises us one thing and reality reveals its opposite—as Noah is promised no flood will again cover the earth, yet we see that the mighty seas cover the better part of the globe. Scripture, then, against the beliefs cherished by good Christian folk, is no reliable guide to reality. On the other hand, Scripture also remains a repository of certain troubling truths that continue to confront us. If this anonymous harpooned whale, soon to be hauled on board and subjected to the try-works, is evidence of the unfulfilment of Scripture, the whale of all whales in the novel will nevertheless prove to be a worthy avatar of the biblical Leviathan, and in the great closing scene when he destroys the *Pequod* and its crew he will indeed laugh at the shaking of the spear and count darts as stubble. The strong poetry of the speech from the Whirlwind is quoted not merely to be refuted but also to set up a resonance that at the end of the novel will, in Melville's orchestration of voices, find an answering poetry in his description of the devastating power of the whale.

The extended citation of Job creates a biblical force-field in this passage that generates two biblicisms in its brilliant last sentence: "For with the strength of a thousand thighs in his tail, Leviathan had run his head under the mountains of the sea, to hide him from the Pequod's fish-spears." The archaic "hide him" is a small formal signal that the language has moved into a biblical zone.

There is no actual quotation here, but "thighs" is a recurrent biblical synecdoche for potency, whether because it is a site of the strong warrior's bunched muscles or a metonymic euphemism for the male organ. (The two Hebrew words for "thighs" are variously rendered in the King James Version as "loins," "thighs," and even "legs," so the idiom is a little hard to track in translation, though Melville clearly picked up the basic idea of virile power.) The phrase "with the strength of a thousand thighs" is Melville's own mythicizing variation on the biblical idiom, effectively marking the difference of scale between the Leviathan and its human hunters and so contradicting what has just been said about unfulfilments. The "mountains of the sea" seems to refer to the vast masses of water above the head of the plummeting whale, but it is also a reminiscence of the psalm in Jonah (another important biblical book for this novel), in which the depths of the sea are juxtaposed with the roots of mountains: "The waters compassed me about... the depth closed me round about, the weeds were wrapped about my head. I went down to the bottoms of the mountains" (Jonah 2:5–6). Here as elsewhere it is biblical poetry rather than prose that is the prime source for Melville's language. It provides him a set of terms and images with a cosmic or mythic amplitude even as he recasts them in his own distinctive language.

There is, then, a variety of ways in which "that old tongue" of the King James Version of the Bible makes itself heard in Melville's prose. At times, he adopts the diction of the Bible, moving from actual quotation to pseudo-quotation to biblicizing turns of speech. At other moments, whether consciously or not, he picks up in the formal patterns of his prose the semantic parallelism that underlies biblical poetry, using it as an alternate or simultaneous model for epic language along with the dominant English model of blank verse. At a good many junctures, a biblical image or symbol is taken up with no explicit signal pointing to the scriptural text in which it originates and usually with a surprising new spin given to the biblical idea. For Melville there is often a consonance between the language or the imagery of the 1611 translation of the Bible and the great English poetry with which it is contemporaneous. Here is a single, exemplary sentence from a description of a whaling boat desperately caught in a ferocious squall: "The wind increased to a howl; the waves dashed their bucklers together; the whole squall roared, forked, and crackled around us like white fire upon the prairie, in which, unconsumed, we were burning; immortal in the jaws of death" (p. 194). Although the Bible never compares waves to crashing shields, as Melville so boldly and effectively does, "buckler" is redolent of the King James Version of Psalms, where it appears with some frequency as a metaphor for God's protecting power. The sequence "roared, forked, and crackled" is part of the distinctive poetic lexicon of *King Lear*, and these words, accompanied by such overlapping terms as "burst," "buckle," and "crack," recur in the novel to express a world of violent energies that tear things apart (including Ahab's heart). The image of burning unconsumed is of course drawn from the burning bush in Exodus 3, but instead of being a miraculous manifestation of divine fire, it is here a representation of the searing agony of somehow living on in the murderous maw of death. As Melville embraces the biblical image, the pattern of the sentence begins to look like the parallel structure of biblical poetry: "unconsumed, we were burning; immortal in the jaws of death." By and large, the figurative language of the novel is not biblical, because Melville's metaphors express his fondness for conceits, for fantastic elaborations of figurative comparisons. When a biblical image surfaces in a metaphor, as here or as in "the strength of a thousand thighs," it is generally transmuted into Melville's own metaphoric idiom, with its attachment to flaunted paradox and hyperbole.

The recurrent figure of the Leviathan is the best illustration of how Melville is at once profoundly biblical and paradoxically anti-biblical. Scripture as it was perceived by the Christian community from which Melville inwardly set himself apart was for the most part a safe and reassuring book, even as it was already being challenged by geology and archeology (the testimony of both are duly registered in *Moby-Dick*) and historical research. It offered a neat and delimited time frame for creation—not much more than five thousand years, as Melville reminds us—together with promises of God's providential concern for humankind and the delineation of an orderly plan of redemption history. All this Melville categorically rejected, and in Leviathan he discovered a kind of hole in the fabric of Scripture opening up into the shadowy vastness of a pre-scriptural reality. Leviathan derives from the sphere of myth—in fact, though Melville could not have known this, from a violent Canaanite creation myth. But if he lived three-quarters of a century before the discovery of the Ugaritic texts that revealed the full mythic lineaments of Leviathan, he clearly intuited the archetypal nature of the beast, associating it with Perseus's sea-monster, St. George's dragon, and other fabled aqueous or amphibian creatures. At one point, he takes pains to invent a variety of terms to indicate an order of time to which Leviathan belongs that utterly shatters the temporal frame of the Bible. Referring to geology, he speaks of "pre-adamite traces in the stereotype plates of nature," and he evokes the primordial antiquity of Leviathan in the following terms:

> Who can show a pedigree like Leviathan? Ahab's harpoon had shed older blood than Pharaoh's. Methuselah seems a schoolboy. I look round to shake hands with Shem. I am horror-struck at this antemosaic, unsourced existence of the unspeakable horrors of the whale, which, having been before all time, must needs exist after all humane ages are over. (p. 380)

The initial question here may have some kinship with the use of rhetorical questions in biblical poetry, as, most memorably, at the beginning of the speech from the Whirlwind. But because the passage expresses a vision of reality antithetical to the biblical one, the language immediately swerves away from any biblical models. Leviathan is older than the Pharaohs, themselves going back to a period a millennium and a half before the Bible. The Bible's own Primeval History is evoked in jocular-colloquial terms, while at the same time cast in the form of biblical parallelism: "Methuselah seems a schoolboy. I look round to shake hands with Shem." The notion of geologic time, which Melville manages to coordinate with mythic time, referring earlier in this same paragraph to "ante-chronical Leviathans," opens up an abyss of "unspeakable horrors" because it drops the bottom out of history, leaving man as an inconsequential and transient mote in a play of cosmic energies that vastly antedates him and that will no doubt outlast him. It is as though Melville, by introducing the dimension of endless time, had taken the difficult vision of the voice from the Whirlwind, in which man is relegated to the sidelines of the teeming panorama of creation, and raised it to a second power that makes it still more unsettling for an anthropocentric view of existence. For this radical project, he enlists, as we have seen, biblical gestures, the familiarity of ordinary American speech, moments of high-poetic diction, and an easy freedom to coin new words. The innovative character of the style and the boldly heterodox viewpoint are inseparable.

Before Melville shattered the stylistic molds in *Moby-Dick*, the prose of American fiction had by and large been a rather awkward emulation of British models. The extravagant stylistic hybridity of *Moby-Dick* is a thoroughly American synthesis, even in the way it taps resources from the literature of seventeenth-century England. Let me suggest tentatively that there is a relation between the horizon of possibilities of style and class structure. The assumption of a decorum of literary style—Melville, of course, is creatively indecorous, like many American novelists after him—is ultimately linked with social hierarchy. That is to say, a tacit sense that there is an educated class that models the norms of linguistic propriety for the culture as a whole quietly imposes certain constraints on literary usage. This hardly means that everybody writes the same way, but it does encourage individual writers to observe the norms of propriety in their prose, however differently they do it. In this regard it scarcely matters whether the writer has a university degree (the British university being a zone of male social privilege till well into the twentieth century) or is home-educated (Jane Austen) or chiefly self-educated (Dickens). In this system, it is still possible for a novelist to create a highly idiosyncratic style, as the zany prose of Laurence Sterne suggests, but this is no more than the exception that proves the rule. There is no real Sternian tradition in English prose because there is not sufficient cultural latitude for the emergence of such a tradition. In respect to style, though only to style, the famous pronouncement of Dr. Johnson, that great enforcer of decorums in English criticism, about *Tristram Shandy*, seems right: "Nothing odd will last."

The eccentricities of Melville's style, on the other hand, are rooted in American experience. He is the product of a society that was in some ways still inchoate. It would be naïve to imagine that there were no class distinctions, and of course a ship's crew is itself a hierarchical structure, with its ladder of officers and its common seamen. But there was no precise American equivalent to the established class structure in England—Faulkner would remind us how poor white trash could turn itself overnight into a kind of aristocracy—and hence there was no firm social matrix for the expectation of linguistic propriety in literature. Though by the mid-nineteenth century, there were in fact palpable distinctions of class in America (and American democracy, of course, had been from the outset a democracy conceived for propertied white males), these lacked the clearly defined contours and the sense of insuperable social obstacles of a hereditary class system. And, whatever the social realities, the cherished myth of a classless society was potent, enabling, among other effects, writers to undertake things that would not have been readily feasible elsewhere.

The elements of fluidity in the American situation had linguistic consequences. The spoken American language by mid-nineteenth century was already a new and different thing from its British counterpart, as Melville's keen ear told him. The pronounced biblical trend in American culture, which in some sectors of the population even affected speech, opened a stratum of the language for literary use that in England was in the process of being closed off. Melville's own huge and distinctively American ambition, poorly understood by his contemporaries, to fuse poetry and prose, epic and tragedy and novel, led him to combine colloquial and biblical, Shakespearian and Miltonic, with the ambling language of a learned encyclopedist thrown in for good measure. There is little sense of hierarchy in all these constituents of his prose as he assumed, rightly or not, that there was little sense of hierarchy in the society that was its setting. No one after Melville wrote very much like him, but he established a precedent for later American novelists in the bustling promiscuity with which he mingled high and low, modern and archaic, with a strong biblical thread running through the pattern. Once a model this powerful becomes part of the ongoing literary tradition, it continues to make its presence felt in unanticipated ways. Several prominent British writers, for example, have expressed admiration for Saul Bellow's style (especially in tributes after Bellow's death), sometimes with a wistful sense that there is nothing quite like it in England. Although *The Adventures of Augie March* exhibits an obvious affiliation with Mark Twain, the flamboyant heterogeneity of Bellow's prose in this novel and elsewhere surely owes something to Melville's precedent as well. What Melville set out to do at the beginning of the 1850s must have seemed a little crazy and, indeed, was condemned as crazy by some of his critics. After the fact, it looks more like the powerful stylistic realization of a possibility inherent in American culture, and it would have momentous consequences for the subsequent course of the language of American fiction.

Chapter 3

∾

Absalom, Absalom!
Lexicon

*F*aulkner's deep engagement in the Bible, and, as he himself stressed, especially in the Hebrew Bible, is well known, but whether it impinged on the extravagantly idiosyncratic texture of his writing is not altogether clear. He claimed that he read all the way through the King James Version every ten or twelve years in the fourteen-volume edition that sat on his shelves. He listed the Old Testament together with Dickens, Conrad, Cervantes, Balzac, and a few others among the books he had loved as a young man and to which he returned as to old friends. In his 1956 *Paris Review* interview, he said of his own writing, "Mine is the standard which has to be met, which is when the work makes me feel the way I do when I read *La Tentation de Saint Antoine*, or the Old Testament, they make me feel good."[1] The juxtaposition of Flaubert's lexically profuse, richly orna-

---

[1] "William Faulkner," an interview with Jean Stein. Reprinted in *William Faulkner: Three Decades of Criticism*, edited by Frederick J. Hoffman and Olga W. Vickery (New York: Harcourt Brace, 1962), p. 72.

mented novel with the spare and concise narratives of the ancient Hebrew writers suggests that he had no general stylistic criterion in mind. What made him feel good about a piece of literature was evidently some indeterminate quality of imaginative authority, a sense of compelling fit between form and meaning. And he must have relished putting together in his interview response the flamboyant expression of Flaubert's hallucinatory Romanticism and the stern, concise narrative of the Hebrew Bible.

Absalom, Absalom!, which is surely one of Faulkner's two or three masterpieces and arguably one of the greatest American novels of the twentieth century, as *Moby-Dick* is of the nineteenth century, throws the question of his relationship with the Bible into sharp focus. It is the only one of his books that uses a phrase from the Bible—it must be said, a slightly modified quotation from the King James Version—as a title. (The title of *Go Down Moses* is a quotation from the Negro spiritual, not from Exodus.) It is also the only one of his novels that is elaborately structured on the scaffolding of a biblical plot—the story of the rape of Tamar by her half-brother Amnon and the subsequent revenge murder of Amnon by her brother Absalom, told in 2 Samuel 13. Despite the importance of the biblical story for Faulkner's novel, which invites some detailed reflection, he scrupulously avoids quoting from it except for the title.

The idea of using an ancient story to structure a novel may well have been suggested to Faulkner by Joyce's use of the Odyssey in *Ulysses*, but what he does with the classic text is significantly different. In Joyce's case, the Odyssey as the "domestic" epic of antiquity did present topics of conjugality, homecoming, and setting the home in order that could be interestingly transposed to the world of an ordinary sensual man in the twentieth century, but in quite a few (though by no means all) of the episodes of *Ulysses* the parallels with the Odyssey are exercises in ingenuity, extended conceits, that are more important for the writer than they are likely to be for most readers. In Faulkner's case, on the other hand, there is a deep and pervasive affinity between the world of his novel and the passion-blighted lethal realm of family, politics, and history represented in the story of David and his children. Before I say anything about how that story may work its way into Faulkner's language, it is worth observing what a penetrating reader he is of the biblical tale, and some attention to his interpretive insights as a reader of Scripture may be more instructive than any mechanical tracing of the parallels between his plot and the one in 2 Samuel.

Faulkner understood far better than all but a few biblical scholars three fundamental aspects of the David story: the moral ambiguity of the character of David; David's tragic fixation on sons, which notably exceeds even the patriarchal norms of the Hebrew Bible; and, above all, the central, painful paradox that the narrative of the founding of the Davidic dynasty is also the story of the fall of the house of David. Let me comment briefly on each of these aspects. Through the hagiographic lens of post-biblical Jewish and Christian interpretation, David was generally seen as the sweet singer of Israel, divinely inspired and divinely elected to be the first in the line that in the end-time would produce the eschatological messiah. (In the original story, the reference of that Hebrew term is strictly political, for it is simply the designation of the legitimate anointed king, the *mashiaḥ*.) Medieval iconography characteristically represents him as a bearded sage with a crown, playing the harp. The biblical writer, on the other hand, presents David as a man who sometimes emphatically declares himself to be innocent (as Sutpen is said to be) but who also seems quite calculating, using women in particular as instruments to power, and who is prepared to do almost anything to survive and achieve his destiny to rule—pretending to be a drooling madman before the king of Gath, serving as vassal to Israel's archenemies the Philistines, massacring whole towns of Amalekites, often yielding, whether helplessly or not we cannot be sure, to his murderous henchman Joab. He repeatedly disavows any responsibility for the sundry deaths of Saul's offspring, but the writer allows at least a shadow of ambiguity to hover over these protestations. What Quentin's grandfather, who was Sutpen's confidant, at least in one episode, says of this enigmatic figure could easily apply to his biblical model, David: *"Given the occasion and the need, this man can and will do anything."*[2] (The italics are Faulkner's.) When Sutpen, emerging from the church with his new bride, is pelted with clods and refuse by the townspeople, we are expected to recall Shimei's pelting the fleeing David with dirt and stones (2 Samuel 16), but we should equally remember that Shimei, a member of Saul's tribe of Benjamin, also denounces David as a "bloody man," a "man of Belial," epithets that David, like Sutpen, might conceivably deserve.

[2]William Faulkner, *Absalom, Absalom!* (New York: Vintage, 1986), p. 35.

The biblical David is obsessed with sons, which seems to be both a matter of spontaneous paternal affection—not much in evidence in the case of Sutpen—and of preoccupation with establishing a dynasty. There is a painfully poignant moment in the David story that, even with no trace of quotation, resonates profoundly through Faulkner's novel. After the assassination of Amnon, a false report is brought to David "saying, Absalom hath slain all the king's sons, and there is not one of them left" (2 Samuel 13:30), and David is flung into utter despair. The report is then dismissed by the courtier Jonadab, who nevertheless contrives to repeat twice the ominous phrase "all the king's sons are dead" in the process of denying it. That very specter of the death of all the sons of the would-be founder of the dynasty, picked up from the biblical narrative, haunts the second half of the story of Thomas Sutpen. Faulkner's protagonist, moreover, like the biblical hero, becomes estranged from the son he needs to love. When Absalom returns from exile, he gets no more than a cold formal kiss from his father, who continues to keep him at arm's length. It is this above all that drives Absalom to a rebellious rage that leads him to usurp the throne and threaten his father's life. In the novel, Charles Bon, otherwise the parallel to Amnon, is very much like the biblical Absalom in wanting the one thing from his father that Sutpen will not give him—recognition as his son.

Finally, though the biblical story strains to be a tale of triumph, capped by David's grand victory hymn near the end, it is riven with intimations of disaster and doom. The direct consequence of David's adultery with Bathsheba and his murder of her husband Uriah is the denunciation of the king by the prophet Nathan, which is not only a strong piece of moral castigation but the pronouncement of a terrible curse: "Wherefore hast thou despised the commandment of the LORD, to do evil in his sight?... Now therefore the sword shall never depart from thine house; because thou hast despised me.... Behold, I will raise up evil against thee out of thine own house" (2 Samuel 12:9–11). What Faulkner firmly grasped about the biblical story is that the force of this curse is never really dispelled. Its enactment begins immediately in the next chapter with the rape of Tamar, followed by the murder of Amnon, then Absalom's flight and his eventual rebellion with full intent to kill his father. Even at the very end, as David lies on his deathbed, his sons struggle for the succession, and as David is aware in his mafioso-like last testament to Solomon, the throne of his successor will be secured only through the shedding of blood. All this becomes a deeply relevant background of reference for the story of Sutpen's blighted dream of dynasty, complicated by the preoccupation with race, even if Sutpen's succession, unlike David's, will be irrevocably cut off. And in Sutpen's case, too, evil is raised up against him from his own house.

The profound interinvolvement of text and intertext in *Absalom, Absalom!* through a shared vision of character and history is not accompanied by any pronounced biblicizing tendency in Faulkner's style. (There are, it should be said, two general styles in Faulkner's fiction, the labyrinthine-poetic and the pungently vernacular, but the latter is not much in evidence in *Absalom, Absalom!* apart from brief snippets in the dialogues.) It would seem that Faulkner's prose, unlike Melville's, is intrinsically resistant to the assimilation of elements of biblical style because all its most distinctive traits are antithetical to biblical prose or poetry as it is represented in the King James Version.

The spectacular peculiarities of Faulkner's style are familiar to all his readers, but a brief summary of them here may be helpful. Conrad Aiken's vivid description of Faulkner's style in 1939, just three years after the publication of *Absalom, Absalom!* and ten years after the appearance of *The Sound and the Fury*, has never been surpassed:

> The exuberant and tropical luxuriance of sound which Jim Europe's jazz band used to exhale, like a jungle of rank creepers taking place before one's eyes,—magnificently and endlessly interinvolved, glisteningly and ophidianly in motion, coil sliding over coil, and leaf and flower forever magically interchanging,—was scarcely more bewildering, in its sheer inexhaustible fecundity, than Mr. Faulkner's style.[3]

In the case of Melville, who shares Faulkner's fondness for stylistic extravagance and for stretching the lexical limits of the English language (*Absalom, Absalom!* includes such terms as "abnegant," "unmeditant," "unamaze," "undefeat," "random" as a noun, "abrupt" as a verb), the adhesion to the rhetorical strategies of biblical poetry, as we have seen, leads to paratactic moves that sometimes are quite biblical. Faulkner's syntax, on the other hand, is spectacularly hypotactic, spinning out, as Aiken's image suggests, in complicated coils that allow

[3]Conrad Aiken, "William Faulkner: The Novel as Form," *Atlantic Monthly*, November 1939, p. 650.

nothing like the orderly march of independent clauses and parallel statements that characterizes biblical writing. In extreme contrast to the spare line of biblical prose, he gives us, as Aiken goes on to say, "a persistent offering of obstacles, a calculated system of screens and obtrusions, of confusions and ambiguous interpolations and delays," all of which, on the level of the characteristically serpentine sentence, provide a microcosmic image of the structure of the novels themselves.

Faulkner is famously fond of polysyllabic and recondite terms, many of them abstractions (again, in contradistinction to the Bible): immemorial, indomitable, impervious, implacable, immolation, apotheosis, avatar, abnegation, coruscation, fortitude, succubus, and many more of the same. In *Absalom, Absalom!* what is often predominant in the vocabulary is a series of terms indicating fluidity, insubstantiality, and elusiveness: effluvium, illusion, dream, ghosts, wraith, "nebulous suspension"; and, to cite the language used at one point about the fine New Orleans clothes of Charles Bon's strange son who comes to live at Sutpen's Hundred, it was "as if they had been woven of chimaeras or of smoke" (p. 160). All these terms obviously bear on the maddeningly elusive, mesmerizingly spectral nature of the past in the novel, which constantly haunts its heirs in 1909, obsesses them, yet remains finally inaccessible and irreducibly ambiguous. Against this pervasive language of flow and evanescence, a set of biblical terms insistently recurs in the novel that is both a counterweight and a crucial focus of meaning. The King James Version enters into Faulkner's otherwise antithetical prose not as a stylistic strategy but as a thematic lexicon.

The recurrent biblical terms in *Absalom, Absalom!*, which I shall list either as single items or, where relevant, as clusters of overlapping terms, are: birthright, curse, land or earth, name and lineage, get (as a noun, an archaic term for "offspring" generally restricted in modern usage to animal breeding, which is in part why Faulkner likes to use it for humans, though the biblical "begat" also influences him), sons or seed, birthplace, inheritance, house, flesh and blood (used as both the idiomatic hendiadys and as isolated items), bones (often in conjunction with flesh), dust and clay (both of these in the biblical sense of images for man's mortal and finite condition). A consideration of each of these thematically fraught terms should clarify how the writing in this novel is pervasively biblical even as a conspicuously unbiblical syntax and vocabulary are constantly flaunted.

Dust and clay. The Hebrew Bible conveys the most concrete sense of the material creatureliness of the human condition. The image in Genesis 2 of God's shaping the first man from the soil as a potter shapes clay is never far from the imagination of the ancient Hebrew writers. The curse pronounced on Adam after the eating of the forbidden fruit resonates profoundly through the Hebrew Scriptures: "for dust thou *art*, and unto dust thou shall return" (Genesis 3:19). Faulkner keenly registers this powerfully concrete imagining of human existence. The pertinent biblical terms he taps from it in *Absalom, Absalom!* serve as a kind of ballast for all that repertory of words that point to things floating off, dissolving, turning into dreams or illusions. When Charles Bon, the New Orleans sophisticate, arrives as if out of nowhere at the new Mississippi college where his half-brother Henry is enrolled, he is described as "a personage who in the remote Mississippi of that time must have appeared almost phoenix-like, fullsprung from no childhood, born of no woman and impervious to time and, vanished, leaving no bones nor dust anywhere" (p. 58). Both "bones" and "dust" make full sense here only if they are aligned with their biblical usage, the first as a synecdoche for man's physical being, and the second as an epithet for man's mortal frame or for mortality itself ("for dust thou *art*, and unto dust thou shall return"). In this case, of course, the biblical terms are introduced only to be negated, at least in Mr. Compson's speculative fantasy about Charles Bon. The incidental reference to the phoenix myth is a token of how Greek and biblical allusions intertwine in the novel. (Elsewhere, Faulkner explicitly and repeatedly coordinates the fall of the house of David with the fall of the house of Atreus as it is represented in Aeschylus's *Agamemnon*.) In this fantastic reconstruction, Bon becomes one of those figures from the antebellum past who seems to be more wraith or myth than palpable person—"impervious [that favorite Faulknerian word] to time," "born of no woman" (a reversal of the biblical "man born of woman,"), vanishing with no residue of bones or dust. But as a keenly attentive reader of the Bible, Faulkner knew that bones, dust, flesh and blood, are ineluctable, that all the extravagant fantasies spun out by convoluted consciousness are pulled back to the sheer materiality of mortal existence that is our human fate and of which the ancient Hebrew writers were so acutely aware.

A particularly vivid instance is the elderly Rosa Coldfield's recollection of the long-ago moment when she attained puberty. It must be said that this virtuoso prose performance is not intrinsically related to the central concerns of the novel but, like a good many other passages in Faulkner, reads like an improvised riff on a theme the writer has picked up as he goes (Conrad Aiken's analogy with jazz is especially apt for moments like this). Rosa is remembering her fourteenth spring, *"the spring and summertime which is every female's who breathed above dust, beholden of all betrayed springs held over from all irrevocable time, repercussed, bloomed again"* (p. 115). Rosa's sense of sharing the female condition with all women born is nicely registered in the biblical "who breathed above dust" ("breath" and "breathing" are of course biblical idioms for life), but this fundamental perception is complicated and perhaps hopelessly obscured by the unbiblical notion that all such springs are somehow compacted together, "repercussed," eternally retained from time that is "irrevocable" (still another favorite Faulkner word). The element of betrayal in all springs may derive from the fact that Rosa's sexual readiness is to remain forever unconsummated. A few lines down, Rosa, having declared that no man had looked on her as "female flesh," goes on to assert her biological heritage as woman in an interplay of different dictions and frames of reference that is characteristic of Faulkner's writing:

> *But root and urge I do insist and claim, for had I not heired too from all the unsistered Eves since the Snake? Yes, urge I do: warped chrysalis of what blind perfect seed: for who shall say what gnarled forgotten root might not bloom yet with some globed concentrate*

more globed and concentrate and heady-perfect be-
cause the neglected root was planted warped and lay
not dead but merely slept forgot.

After a brandishing of polysyllabic terms—both "pre-
dacious" and "intimidate" as an adjective appear in the
immediately preceding sentence—Faulkner creates a
stylistic counterpoint in this sentence, which concludes
a long paragraph, where monosyllabic words predominate. This move is both biblical and something quite
different. "Root" is a key recurrent term in the Bible, as
is "seed," but both function in a second frame of reference here that is strictly biological, as the mention of
"chrysalis" (the only word in the sentence besides "concentrate" and "neglected" that has more than two syllables) instructs us. The Garden story is explicitly invoked, but, oddly, Eve's seducer is referred to as the
Snake, not the Serpent, perhaps to express the animal
immediacy of the idea for Rosa but also for the sake of
the rhythm. (Iambic cadences dominate the sentence as
much as in any passage from *Moby-Dick*.) What "globed
concentrate" refers to is not entirely clear—nectar, dew,
liquid fertilizer, semen are all possibilities. In any case,
the root, warped or sleeping, and the female breathing
above dust insist, through all the bewilderments of syntax and imagery, that this woman, destined to desicca-
tion and isolation, shares a fate of physical creatureliness first defined for our culture in Genesis.

"Clay" occurs less frequently in the novel than "dust,"
and much less frequently than "flesh," but has the same
valence of meaning. An early characterization of Sutpen
joins a reference to "his own fallible judgment" with
"mortal clay" (p. 41). More vividly, Rosa reports being

physically blocked by Clytie in these terms: *"I stopped in running's midstride again though my body, blind unsentient barrow of deluded clay and breath, still advanced"* (p. 114). The juxtaposition of terms here concisely illustrates how Faulkner joins together his own stylistic and figurative predilections with biblical terms. The image of the barrow has no biblical affiliation, and "unsentient" is pure Faulknerian—note his love for words with negative prefixes—but the clay and breath are straight out of the King James Version, affirming Rosa's sense that she is, after all, a carnal and mortal creature, not one of the phantasmagoric figures that people this story told again and again.

Flesh and blood, flesh and bones. Yielding flesh, hard bone, and fluid blood are imagined in the Bible as the primary constituents of the human body. "Flesh" is very often a synecdoche in biblical usage for living creature or human being—thus God says to Noah, "The end of all flesh is come before me" (Genesis 6:13). The idiomatic collocation "flesh and blood" is not actually biblical, though it is common in rabbinic Hebrew, perhaps as an extrapolation from biblical usage. Flesh does combine with bone in a biblical idiom that stresses the strong physicality of kinship, as in Laban's words to his nephew Jacob, "Surely thou *art* my bone and my flesh" (Genesis 29:14); and in Job 2:5 it is a vivid synecdoche for the human body, "touch his bone and his flesh." Faulkner appears to have taken note of that biblical usage, because "flesh" is joined with "bone" a good deal more often than with "blood" in the novel. The three terms in shifting combinations significantly recur at least twenty times in the book. It is scarcely necessary to track all the occurrences, but a quick consideration of a few strategic instances suggests that for Faulkner these terms are not formulaic epithets for humanity but a way of expressing the irreducible physical agency of every human life. Thus, when Sutpen returns exhausted from four years on the battlefields of the Civil War, we are told, *"He did not pause, did not take that day or two to let the bones and flesh of fifty-nine recuperate,"* not speaking of the war and acting as though *"no flesh and blood of his [had] to suffer by it"* (p. 130). The sundry narrators of *Absalom, Absalom!*, with only minor variations, share the same language, and so it is not surprising that just a little later Quentin's roommate Shreve echoes Mr. Compson's formulation in reconstructing the story: "[he] could would and did breed him two children to find and shield both in themselves and in their progeny the brittle bones and tired flesh of an old man against the day the Creditor would run him to earth for the last time...." (pp. 145–46). Here it is noteworthy that the fixed terms of the hendiadys "bone and flesh" are broken out from the idiomatic collocation and physically vivified through the adjectives "brittle" and "tired." The same paired terms stand out strikingly in the story of how Sutpen faced down the rebelling slaves in Haiti, imposing his terrific presence on them, "bearing more than they believed any bones and flesh could or should (should, yes: to find flesh to stand more than flesh should be asked to stand)" (p. 205).

Repeatedly, one or more of these three biblical bodily terms serves to anchor the illusory evanescent shapes of the haunting past in palpably concrete reality. Mr.

Compson, reflecting on the process through which the heirs to that past attempt to decipher the figures that inhabited it, observes: "we see dimly people, the people in whose living blood and seed we ourselves lay dormant and waiting, in this shadowy attenuation of time possessing now heroic proportions,... impervious to time and inexplicable" (p. 80). The counterpoint between "blood and seed" on the one hand and "shadowy attenuation" on the other says a great deal about the world of fraught antitheses of this novel. "Seed," of course, is another salient biblical term, at once semen and offspring, and it leads to another thematic vector that we shall presently pursue. Toward the end of the novel, as Quentin and Shreve try to imagine what the fated siblings, Judith, Henry, and Bon, might have felt just before the fratricide, they are said to think, *"the three of us are just illusions that he begot, and your illusions are a part of you like your bones and flesh and memory"* (p. 277). The pairing of bones and flesh with illusions and memory creates a kind of double zeugma: what is purely mental and perhaps finally insubstantial is locked together with the palpable physical constituents of the body. In precisely this connection, Charles Bon several times tries to conceive his relationship with his half-brother and with the inaccessible father they share in the same language: *"what cannot I do with this willing flesh and bone if I wish, this flesh and bone and spirit which stemmed from the same source that mine did"* (p. 254); and a moment later he imagines what his father bequeathed him as running "in shadow," a recurrent term in the novel that overlaps with "illusion" and "wraith."

There is one heavily underscored fragment of encoun-

ter in the novel that focuses these repeated concerns with
the flesh and how they bear on the issue of race as well
as of kinship. When Rosa hurries out to the Sutpen estate after Henry has shot Bon, her rush up the stairs to
find out whatever lies in the bedroom is broken when
Clytie, Sutpen's daughter by a slave woman, grabs hold
of her. She is shocked by

> that black arresting and untimorous hand on my white
> woman's flesh. Because there is something in the touch
> of flesh with flesh that abrogates, cuts sharp and straight
> across the devious intricate channels of decorous order-
> ing, which enemies as well as lovers know because it
> makes them both:—touch and touch of that which is
> the citadel of the central I-Am's private own: not spirit,
> soul; the liquorish and ungirdled mind is anyone's to
> take in any darkened hallway of this earthly tenement.
> But let flesh touch flesh, and watch the fall of all the
> eggshell shibboleth of caste and color too. (pp. 111–12)

Note the interplay between the elaborately figurative
("the devious intricate channels," the "darkened hall-
way of this earthly tenement") and the hyper-literalism
of "flesh," which is not even synecdoche here but the
immediate tactile thing itself. There is a parallel interplay of dictions between a high-poetic language with
Shakespearian touches worthy of Melville ("the liquor-
ish and ungirdled mind") and the unadorned monosyllabic "flesh," with its antecedents in biblical idiom. In
this instance, "flesh" brings to earth ballooning illusions
of another sort—the illusion of solipsistic isolation, of a
self forever inaccessible to the other, in which most of
the characters in the novel dwell; and the historically

corrupting and murderous illusion of race, the idea that there is an ontological chasm between people of different pigmentation who in fact touch, couple, breed, and share the same fleshly humanity.

The key terms we have looked at so far address the human condition as such and give Faulkner a way of counterposing the ineluctable reality of the body to the "ungirdled mind" that spins out the convoluted narrative strands of this novel. But in *Absalom, Absalom!* he is centrally concerned with the intertwined issues of family, history, and the fate of the land, and for all these the Old Testament—Genesis and Deuteronomy as much as Samuel—provided him a lexicon that he could introduce into his own very different language as a set of crucial thematic nodes. The ancient Hebrew narratives do not imagine a kingdom about to come that will end history or radically transform it but rather the enactment of God's purposes through a covenanted people in a particular land within the frame of history. This is an idea, as I noted at the outset of this study, that the early generations of English settlers in America embraced and made profoundly their own. Faulkner's novel aims to come to grips with this idea and to show how in the American South it was catastrophically perverted. Thus, his deployment of a biblical lexicon defines the terrible failure of a peculiarly American dream.

Land and curse. In the Hebrew Bible, the land is the theater in which God bestows blessing on His chosen people, but it is equally the place where, if the people betray the covenant, "thy heaven that *is* over thy head shall be brass, and the earth that *is* under thee *shall be* iron. The LORD shall make the rain of thy land powder and dust: from heaven shall it come down upon thee, until thou be destroyed" (Deuteronomy 28:23–24). The next verse, which is directly relevant to the fate of the American South, speaks of Israel's being devastated by its enemies. In keeping with the general avoidance of direct quotation of the Bible in Faulkner's novel, these words are never cited, but, as we shall see, the vision of history they express haunts the book, coalescing around the term "land." In the opening pages, Quentin, exasperated after his first visit with Rosa Coldfield, asks his father: "What is it to me that the land or the earth or whatever it was got tired of him at last and turned and destroyed him? What if it did destroy her family too?" And then he enlarges the scope of destruction in a way that is perfectly consonant with Deuteronomy's specter of total national catastrophe: "It's going to turn and destroy us all someday, whether our name happens to be Sutpen or Coldfield or not" (p. 7).

The conjunction of land and curse is firmly established by the writer in the first dozen pages of the novel because it is the interpretive frame in which the history of the South is seen. The land in its spectacular fecundity, like the biblical land flowing with milk and honey, is a divine gift, but the lust for wealth and power fulfilling itself through the historical crime of slavery violates the gift, bringing down the implacable curse. Rosa marvels over the fact that Sutpen first discovered her sister Ellen, his future bride, of all places in a church.

> In a church, mind you, as though there were a fatality
> and curse on our family and God Himself were seeing

to it that it was performed and discharged to the last drop and dreg. Yes, fatality and curse on the South and on our family as though because some ancestor of ours had elected to establish his descent in a land primed for fatality and already cursed with it, even if it had not been our family, our father's progenitors, who had incurred the curse and had been coerced by Heaven into establishing itself in the land and the time already cursed. (p. 14)

These words, of course, like all the words of this novel, are pronounced by a character, and we need not assume that Faulkner himself subscribed to this theological theory of historical causation. (Rosa, we should recall, was raised by a stern Baptist father.) But the theological framework, plausibly appropriate for most of the Southern characters, gives Faulkner a powerful instrument to articulate a morally driven vision of historical doom in keeping with the grimmest passages of Deuteronomy. One should note that the biblical term "curse" is bracketed here in insistent repetition with "fatality," a Latinate word and a Greek concept alien to the Bible. The coordination of the two terms mirrors lexically the coordination of the stories of David and Agamemnon. In Rosa's speculation, God Himself coerces (or perhaps, tricks) her ancestors into settling this land where the curse will unfold—again, a Greek idea rather than a Hebrew one. But her chain of thought emphatically concludes with the biblical theme and language of the curse on the land, and at the end of this same paragraph she wonders what terrible crime might have been committed by her forebears and Sutpen's that could have demanded this expiation of inexorable destruction—the visiting of the sins of the fathers on their sons.

The curse is implemented through the fierce, unyielding assertion of will and the harboring of resentment and simmering hatred between kin; these are, of course, preeminently biblical themes, though in the novel they are complicated and actually motivated by the fixation on race. After Mr. Coldfield shuts himself up in his house in ultimate protest against the war, as he watches the troops marching by, "he would open the bible and declaim in a harsh loud voice even above the sound of the tramping feet, the passages of the old violent vindictive mysticism which he had already marked" (p. 64). One may forgive Faulkner the imprecision of "mysticism," which has a nice ring here, even if what it refers to is more like unswerving devoutness or theological thinking, but the stubbornness of character, the violence, the unforgiving sentiments transfer readily enough from the marked pages of Mr. Coldfield's Old Testament (it is surely the Old Testament) to the world of this novel. We are not told which biblical passages he declaims, but the oracles of doom in the Prophets, the great catalogue of curses in Deuteronomy, and the David story itself would all be prime candidates for his reading.

The biblical idea of the Promised Land is not directly used in the novel, but there is an intimation that the New World as it has been exploited by the white settlers is an Eden fatally violated. Two-thirds of the way through the novel, when we finally learn about Sutpen's watershed experience as an overseer of slaves in the West Indies, Faulkner, through the intermediary of Quentin's grandfather, spectacularly describes Haiti as a mirror image of the American South, only sharper and more extreme. This passage brings to a brilliant climax the themes of land and curse, to which, as we shall see, it joins the term "blood," powerfully used here in another of its biblical senses—guilt for crimes of violence. The passage deserves quoting at length. This fecund island, Grandfather says, was a place

> where high mortality was concomitant with the money and the sheen on the dollars was not from gold but from blood—a spot of earth which might have been created and set aside by Heaven itself, Grandfather said, as a theatre for violence and injustice and bloodshed and all the satanic lusts of human greed and cruelty, for the last despairing fury of all the pariah-interdict and all the doomed—a little island set in a smiling and fury-lurked and incredible indigo sea, which was the halfway point between what we call the jungle and what we call civilization, halfway between the dark inscrutable continent from which the black blood, the black bones and flesh and thinking and remembering and hopes and desires were ravished by violence, and the cold known land to which it was doomed, the civilized land and people which had expelled some of its own blood and thinking and desires that had become too crass to be faced and borne longer, and set it homeless and desperate on the lonely ocean—a little lost island in a latitude which would require ten thousand years of equatorial heritage to bear its climate, a soil manured with black blood from two hundred years of oppression and exploitation until it sprang with an incredible paradox of

greenery and crimson flowers and sugar cane sapling size and three times the height of a man and a little bulkier of course but valuable pound for pound almost with silver ore, as if nature held a balance and kept a book and offered a recompense for the torn limbs and outraged hearts even if man did not, the planting of nature and man too watered not only by the wasted blood but breathed over by the winds in which the doomed ships had fled in vain, out of which the last tatter of sail had sunk into the blue sea, along with the last vain despairing cry of woman or child had blown away;— the planting of men too: the yet intact bones and brains in which the old unsleeping blood that had vanished into the earth they trod still cried out for vengeance. (pp. 201–2)

No American writer, white or black, has written more wrenching prose than this to convey the foundational crime of slavery in the New World. Against Faulkner's general practice of proliferating often bewildering abstractions, the language is remarkably concrete, beginning with the image of the gold dollars whose sheen derives from blood. The crucial connection repeatedly made is between blood and earth—not at all in the fascist sense but rather in the strict biblical sense. The biblical text that confirms that connection and that informs this entire passage, even though it is only obliquely quoted, is the murder of Abel by Cain. "What hast thou done?" God demands of Cain. "The voice of thy brother's blood crieth unto me from the ground. And now *art* thou cursed from the earth which hath opened her mouth to receive thy brother's blood from thy hand"

(Genesis 4:10–11). (The Hebrew original would have been even more to Faulkner's purpose because the same Hebrew word, 'adamah, is used when the King James Version shows "ground" and then "earth," and it actually means "soil," the raw material from which the first man was fashioned.) The constellation of blood, curse, and earth or soil is explicitly established in these two verses from Genesis 4. Behind the passage in Faulkner, one also senses the presence of God's stern words to Noah after the Flood: "Whoso sheddeth man's blood, by man shall his blood be shed: for in the image of God made he man" (Genesis 9:6). This particular verse might be thought of as the ground upon which the narrative structure is erected in which all of the Sutpens will perish violently. Blood is also joined here, as we saw it joined elsewhere, with bones and flesh; and, in characteristic Faulknerian fashion, these concrete manifestations of the bodily existence of man are linked in an extended zeugma, with no syntactic differentiation, that yokes phenomena of the mind and the emotions: "the black blood, the black bones and flesh and thinking and re-membering and hopes and desires." The predominant image, however, is of the earth irrigated by the blood of the slaves—"the earth which hath opened her mouth to receive thy brother's blood"—an idea Faulkner expresses as "manuring" the soil with black blood, a brilliant con-cisely metaphorical representation of how all this wealth of sugar crops was obtained through the brutal exploita-tion of slave labor. The archetypal nature of the story of Cain and Abel beautifully serves these thematic pur-poses. (In still another coordination of Greek myth and the Bible, the planting of men in the soil out of which wealth springs also recalls, with a kind of inversion, the planting of dragon's teeth out of which warriors sprang.) The brothers Cain and Abel are the first human offspring; their equally shared humanity is conspicuous; and the first violent crime of man against man is fratricide. Slavery is imagined as a kind of fratricide, the shedding of a black man's blood by his white brother, and it will indirectly lead to actual fratricide in the Sutpen family. (In this connection, one should note that Faulkner, who at some moments may seem to be perpetuating certain stereotypes about blacks, is utterly clear on the cultural prejudice of "what we call the jungle and what we call civilization.") The last words of the passage I have excerpted climactically resonate most fully with the biblical story of the first murder and come closest to an actual quotation from it: "the old unsleeping blood that had vanished into the earth they trod still cried out for vengeance." This is a striking instance of Faulkner's procedure of allusion or quasi-allusion through the borrowing of elements of vocabulary rather than through quotation. After the banishment from Eden comes the shedding of blood. Here, a place that might have been an Eden is transformed into a virtual slaughterhouse in the relentless pursuit of profit. Earth, blood, and curse are drawn together in the very conjunction laid out in Genesis. And the idea of the perversion of the New Eden by the settlers of the Americas is a small but revelatory instance of how Faulkner not only is responding to the Bible itself but also is challenging a tradition of American interpretation of the Bible that goes back to the Puritans.

Son, seed, and birthright. In Hebrew Scripture, where there is no world except this one, the only perpetuity, a kind of immortality, that a person can attain is through the begetting of sons (sons and not daughters because of the patrilineal definition of social units). This urgency is felt by women as well as by men, as the desperate cases of Rachel and of the Tamar of Genesis show. In Genesis, as in Faulkner's novel, the propagation of sons is a precarious enterprise, its success repeatedly threatened. The story of the Binding of Isaac is terrifying not only because of the intrinsically ghastly idea of child sacrifice but also because Abraham seems on the verge of cutting off his only male seed by his legitimate wife, the son he has waited for through so many barren decades. And David's story, as we have seen, is haunted by the frightening prospect that all the king's sons may have been killed and hence his dream of dynasty extinguished. The biblical term for offspring, "seed," literally and appropriately rendered in the King James Version, underscores the biological continuity between father and son. And in the biblical dialogues, when a man refers to his child as "my son," the term bears a special weight of affection. Thus, Abraham responds to Isaac's question as the two make their way together up Mount Moriah, "My son, God will provide himself a lamb for the burnt offering" (Genesis 21:8). And in the crucial intertext for Faulkner's novel, David, in a paroxysm of paternal grief, stammers, "O my son Absalom, my son, my son Absalom! would God I had died for thee, O Absalom, my son, my son!" (2 Samuel 18:33).

"Son," of course, is one of the most common words in the English language, and so one should not automatically assume that its recurrence in *Absalom, Absalom!* owes anything to the King James Version. At several points, however, Faulkner introduces it in a way that underscores the link with the Bible. Thus, early in the book, Quentin's father says of Sutpen that from the start he had "a fixed goal in his mind" which was "not the vindication of a past affront in the person of a son whose seed is not yet, and would not be for years yet, planted" (p. 40). The joining of "son" with its virtual biblical synonym "seed," and the reference to the as yet unplanted seed as an image of posterity, coming from a character by no means inclined to biblicisms, are strong indications that this ordinary word carries with it in this novel a freight of biblical connotations and therefore means something different than it does, say, in *Tom Jones* or in *Dombey and Son*. Much later, this adhesion to Hebrew Scripture in the use of "son" is picked up by Shreve during his late-night conversation with Quentin in an extravagant quasi-biblical improvisation:

who should do the paying if not his [Sutpen's] sons, his get, because wasn't it done that way in the old days? the old Abraham full of years and weak and incapable now of further harm, caught at last and the captains and the collectors saying, 'Old man, we dont want you' and Abraham would say, 'Praise the Lord, I have raised about me sons to bear the burden of my iniquities and persecutions; yea, perhaps even to restore my flocks and herds from the hand of the ravisher: that I might rest mine eyes upon my goods and chattels, upon the generations of them and of my descendents increased an hundred fold as my soul goeth out from me.' (p. 260)

This little verbal fantasy is of course a kind of parody of the Old Testament that nevertheless seriously aligns Sutpen's mindset about sons with that of the biblical world. Just a few pages later, when Sutpen encounters Henry during the war (and adamantly refuses to meet with Bon) at an encampment near the front, three spare words of dialogue become the only moment in the story when he expresses what looks like love: "—*Henry, Sutpen says,—My son*" (p. 282). Those two final syllables echo the utterances of a line of biblical fathers who pronounce the selfsame words: Abraham on Mount Moriah, David grieving over the death of Absalom, and even Saul, madly estranged from David, who in their wrenching encounter at the cave of En-gedi, after David has addressed him as "my father," says, in tears, "*Is* this thy voice, my son David?" (1 Samuel 24:16).

In the patrilineal system, the ultimate vocation of the son is to inherit the birthright. Primogeniture dictates that the birthright belongs to the firstborn son, though the Hebrew Bible famously, in a whole series of inventive variations, contrives to subvert this priority. David himself is the youngest of seven sons, and there is no presumption whatever that the successor to his throne will be his firstborn. Charles Bon, Sutpen's firstborn son, who will die at his brother's hand, is categorically excluded from the birthright because in his father's eyes his blood is tainted. Henry, at first siding with his rejected brother, is said to "repudiate his home and birthright" and is later described as having "formally abjured his father and renounced his birthright and the roof under which he had been born" (p. 12, p. 62). (In both these formulations, Faulkner adheres to his procedure of avoiding direct quotation from the Bible: "birthright" is a heavily fraught biblical word, but the legal terms "repudiate" and "renounce" are not biblical, and Esau in Genesis 25:34 is said to have "despised [not 'repudiated'] *his* birthright.") Henry then seals his ineligibility for the birthright by becoming a fratricide and outlaw. Unlike the biblical narratives, where the birthright passes on to an unanticipated son, Faulkner's bleaker tale ends with no son left to inherit the birthright that in any case has become entirely worthless. After everything Thomas Sutpen has built, material and familial, has been utterly devastated, the only survivor is Sutpen's idiot black great-grandson, Jim Bond, who is no more than a pathetic inarticulate witness to the final destruction of Sutpen's Hundred.

House. This is another ordinary word that carries central thematic resonances in the Bible. Its primary meaning as a place of permanent shelter is extended socially in the collocation "father's house" (*beyt 'av*) that indicates the defining kinship unit of the clan, and it is applied politically to mean dynasty. It can also refer either to the palace or the temple. An archeological find that speaks poignantly to the substance of Faulkner's novel preserves the sole extra-biblical mention of a Davidic line—a shard on which only two words appear, *beyt david*, "the house of David." The word "house" variously appears in the novel in conjunction with "birthplace" and "inheritance" and thus is pulled into a biblical semantic orbit. Henry renounces not only birthright but birthplace and house. The grandiose pillared mansion that Sutpen causes to be built, designed by the French

architect he holds in captivity, is the sign and symbol, as
Melville would say, of the perpetual dynasty he means
to establish. By the end of the Civil War, well before its
ultimate destruction, it will be reduced to "a shell ma-
rooned and forgotten in a backwater of catastrophe" (p.
105).

The Hebrew Bible—and especially the Prophets—
troubled by the threatening prospect of historical disaster dictated by Israel's precarious geopolitical location,
abounds in images of houses destroyed, razed "to *even*
the foundation thereof" as Psalm 137 puts it. The term
"house" in its charged biblical sense and the imagery of
the devastation of the house give Faulkner an imaginative vocabulary for the powerful representation of the
catastrophic collapse of the South. When Sutpen, according to Mr. Compson's imaginative reconstruction
of his thinking, becomes aware of the imminent engagement between Bon and Judith, "he must have felt and
heard the design—house, position, posterity and all—
come down like it had been built out of smoke, making
no sound, creating no rush of displaced air and not even
leaving any debris" (p. 215). (This soundless destruction
of the house might be a reversal of the report of the
building of Solomon's temple in 1 Kings 6:7: "there was
neither hammer nor axe *nor* any tool of iron heard in the
house, while it was in building.") The locally striking
image of a design and house built out of smoke is, of
course, a nice intimation of the final disaster in which
the house literally goes up in smoke. It is also very much
in keeping with the way the house—whether palace or
temple or the house of Israel—is imagined by the ancient
Hebrew writers. In contrast to the Odyssey, where the

persistence of the house is never in doubt, only whether it will be rescued from its would-be usurpers, the Bible conceives the house, in its literal and extended senses, as a grand consummation of personal and national destiny that might at any time turn to smoke, should Israel betray the covenant: there is nothing solid or permanent in history that we can count on. That sense of precarious building in a zone of constant fire hazard is deeply inscribed in Faulkner's novel, without, of course, the biblical hope for a restoration of the house.

By the time Quentin and Rosa, accompanied by a deputy sheriff, just before the end of the novel, hurry to the Sutpen mansion, it has long become a macabre thing inwardly collapsing "with a smell of desolation and decay as if the wood of which it was built were flesh" (p. 293). A few minutes later, they see the house engulfed in flame—a vision, with its symbolic historical implications, that becomes a stupendous apocalyptic conclusion to the novel:

> —the three of them staring, glaring at the doomed house: and then for a moment maybe Clytie appeared in that window from which she must have been watching the gates constantly day and night for three months—the tragic gnome's face beneath the clean headrag, against a red background of fire, seen for a moment between two swirls of smoke, looking down at them, perhaps not even now with triumph and no more despair than it had ever worn, possibly even serene above the melting clapboards before the smoke swirled across it again.—and he, Jim Bond, the scion, the last of his race, seeing it too now and howling with human reason now since now even he could have known what he was howling about. (p. 300)

The conflagration that destroys the house Sutpen built also consumes his surviving progeny, his "house" in the extended biblical sense, leaving as survivor and witness only the idiot black great-grandson. In a bitterly ironic comment on Sutpen's dream of dynasty, Jim Bond is called "the scion," a term at once medieval-heraldic and biblical. But the idea of the retarded mixed-race man as the surviving heir is given a dialectical twist in the penultimate paragraph of the novel when Shreve imagines that in due course of time "the Jim Bonds are going to conquer the western hemisphere," only "bleached out," as they spread toward both poles. To which speculative projection Shreve adds a surprising turn: "in a few thousand years, I who regard you will also have sprung from the loins of African kings." Sutpen, the child of hard-scrabble itinerant whites, fiercely set his will to make himself a king, like David. The enduring royalty, however, abides in the once enslaved people brought in captivity from another continent, "sprung from the loins"— an appropriately biblical locution—"of African kings."

The interlinked cluster of thematic terms drawn from the Bible—land, curse, son, birthright, inheritance, house—is thus pulled together in a catastrophic climax in this final scene of fiery destruction, with a compelling correspondence to the biblical plot on which the novel is constructed, a plot, as we have noted, that Faulkner understands as the story of the tragic fall of the house of David. At the same time, there is another biblical text invoked in the novel, more intermittently, and yet with strategic importance for the overarching sense of life that Faulkner articulates. In the case of this other text, moreover, Faulkner occasionally diverges from his general avoidance of quotation. The seemingly innocuous phrase "under the sun" appears with some frequency in the novel, and, taken by itself as an American idiom, there would be no reason to assume that it refers in any way to its biblical source. But when the adolescent Sutpen stumbles upon the existence of hierarchies of class and race, that shocking and illuminating discovery is said to mean more to him "than all the human puny mortals under the sun that might lie in hammocks all afternoon with their shoes off" (p. 192, the confounding vista of a hitherto undreamt-of leisure class being an essential part of his discovery). The generalizing thrust of the phrase "all the human puny mortals" invites the reader to connect the three words that follow with their famous source in Ecclesiastes 1:9: "The thing that hath been, it is *that* which shall be; and that which is done *is* that which shall be done; and *there is* no new *thing* under the sun." Ecclesiastes, moreover, registers its own awareness, akin to Sutpen's, of powerful and oppressive hierarchies: "If thou seest the oppression of the poor, and violent perverting of judgment and justice in a province, marvel not at the matter: for *he that is* higher than the highest regardeth; and *there be* higher than they" (Ecclesiastes 5:8). The cadenced, repetitive insistence of the prose of Ecclesiastes, eloquently rendered in the King James Version, on an unending cycle of futility, at times seems to echo in Faulkner's more syntactically elaborate prose. It certainly can be heard in these characteristically bombastic words of Sutpen, which read like a highfalutin paraphrase of Ecclesiastes: "I learned little save that most of the deeds, good and bad both, incurring opprobrium or plaudits or reward either, within the scope of man's abilities, had already been performed and were to be learned about only from books" (p. 195). Faulkner's invocation of a dissident biblical text is akin to what Melville, quarreling with the providential premises of Christianity, does in his use of the Book of Job. The Bible, after all, is an anthology spanning many centuries and disparate points of view, but its dominant consensus is a hopeful and trusting belief that through divine guidance history is progressing by stages, however difficult, toward a grand fulfillment. Such an idea could scarcely serve Faulkner's somber vision of history and the fate of the South. By reading the David narrative perhaps not against the grain of the original story but certainly against the grain of its predominant Christian and Jewish interpretations, he was able to make this particular book of the Bible rivetingly relevant to the world of his novel. Ecclesiastes provided him a somewhat different opportunity.

This late biblical text is a probing argument against the mainline assumptions of the Hebrew Bible regarding time, history, and value. In Ecclesiastes, things do not move forward purposefully and progressively, as, paradigmatically, creation moves forward from the first day to the seventh, but instead they go round and round. Everything is repeated and nothing lasts; what is wrong cannot be set right, and nothing of value survives: "I have seen all the works that are done under the sun; and, behold, all *is* vanity and vexation of spirit. That which is crooked cannot be made straight: and that which is wanting cannot be numbered" (1:14–15).

This bleak, unblinking outlook accords well with the sense of both the sundry narrators in 1909 and the mid-

nineteenth-century characters in *Absalom, Absalom!*
The South's dream of triumphant advance through history—epitomized in Sutpen—has proved to be an empty
illusion, and after the chain of fatal missteps from the
primal sin of slavery to the defeat of 1865, that which is
crooked will never be made straight. One should note
that whereas the explanation for disaster when the David
story and the Deuternomistic History are recalled in the
novel is theological—"why God let us lose the War"—
the frame of reference of Ecclesiastes is essentially secular, apart from the pious coda added by an editor. Existence is stuck in a miserable rut because that is the nature
of existence. Man is denied the fulfillment of his desires
because human desires are insatiable—"the eye is not
satisfied with seeing nor the ear with hearing" (1:8). One
wonders whether Faulkner may not have had Ecclesiastes in mind as he imagined his protagonist's grand design for Sutpen's Hundred. This is how the first-person
narrator of the biblical text speaks of his life: "I made
me great works; I builded me houses; I planted me vine-
yards: I made me gardens and orchards, and I planted
trees in them of all *kind of* fruits.... I got me servants
and maidens, and had servants born in my house ... and,
behold, all *was* vanity and vexation of spirit, and *there
was* no profit under the sun" (2:4–5, 7, 11).

The resolution that Ecclesiastes proposes in the face
of these cycles of futility is a kind of zero-degree unil-
lusioned hedonism—to enjoy the sensual pleasures of
what is here and now before they vanish: "*it is* good and
comely *for one* to eat and to drink, and to enjoy the
good of all his labour that he taketh under the sun"
(5:18). Charles Bon, growing up in a weirdly shuttered

sybaritic world in New Orleans under the eye of his embittered mother, is imagined formulating for himself a similar view, though it is put more starkly: "he had learned that there were three things and no more: breathing, pleasure, darkness; and that without money there could be no pleasure, and without pleasure it would not even be breathing but mere protoplasmic inhale and collapse of blind unorganism in a darkness where light never began" (p. 240).

The relationship of the prose of this American masterwork to biblical style is highly paradoxical and for that very reason instructive about the possibilities of cross-pollination from one literature to another. The language of Faulkner's novel, with its fondness for arcane and flamboyant terms, its convoluted syntax, and the baroque efflorescence of its metaphors, could scarcely be further from biblical style. Yet the novelist works into his own otherwise antithetical prose key terms culled from the Bible that define the characters, much of their mental world, and above all the historical frame within which they move. In this fashion, the book's prose comes to ring with biblical resonances even though most of its constituents are quite unlike anything in the Bible. And the affinity of outlook with Ecclesiastes establishes another sort of nexus with the Bible. No scriptural text is more hypnotically incantatory than this one, deploying as it does insistent cadenced repetition to convey in poetic prose the sense of a world where everything keeps going round and round, bringing no profit, getting nowhere. The prose of Ecclesiastes is of course not a source of Faulkner's style, but it does encourage his predilection, as the fragmentary citations of Ecclesiastes suggest, for emphatic repetition and incantation, here used to express an analogous vision of futile cyclical movement. *Absalom, Absalom!* is manifestly a modernist novel synthesizing Conrad's impressionist narrative method, in which the story is pieced together in disregard of chronological order through fragments, with Joyce's interiorization of novelistic language. Yet these formally innovative features of literary modernism are coupled in Faulkner's work with a strong sense of the abiding relevance of the age-old biblical tradition, which provides him a special vocabulary to represent history and the moral world. *Absalom, Absalom!*, for all its aggressive modernism, vividly demonstrates how the King James Version of the Bible, three full centuries after the Puritan founders, continued to enrich and distinguish American prose.

Chapter 4

∾

Seize the Day
American Amalgam

*T*he opening words of Saul Bellow's *The Adventures of Augie March* (1953), "I am an American, Chicago-born," are probably one of the most quoted sentences from a twentieth-century American novel. They are usually cited, justly, as an expression of a new cultural pluralism that was emerging in American literature in the period after World War II: Augie, the child of Russian-Jewish immigrants, with his very first words unapologetically flaunts his particular ethnic identity as a vividly authentic embodiment of the multifaceted American self. But it is equally worth observing that Augie's initial affirmation has some bearing as well on the style of this novel and on what the possibilities of an American style might be. In a 1991 interview for *Bostonia Magazine*, Bellow himself emphasizes what *Augie March* meant for him as a stylistic breakthrough: "What I found was the relief of turning away from mandarin English and putting my own accents into the language. My earlier books had been straight and respectable. As if I had to satisfy the demands of H. W. Fowler. But in *Augie March* I wanted to invent a new sort of American sentence. Something like a fusion of colloquialism and elegance.... Street language combined with high style."[1] The street language, of course, was given formal motivation through the use of a first-person narrator, and many of Bellow's subsequent novels and stories would similarly be narrated in a first person that stamped the language with a colloquial liveliness and energy of invention. The precedent of *Huckleberry Finn*, though it uses a very different American vernacular, is surely relevant, and the picaresque form of *Augie March* reinforces the notion that Mark Twain was at least in the back of Bellow's mind.

The linguistic culture of America, Bellow came to recognize a decade into his career, is fluid, quirky, at times extravagantly heterogeneous. "As for us, here in America," the narrator of "Him with His Foot in His Mouth" observes, "we are a demotic, hybrid civilization. We have our virtues but are ignorant of style."[2] What the narrator means by style, as he makes clear in the next sentence, is the unitary, polished, poised style of a Voltaire, a Gibbon, a Saint-Simon. A very different kind of literary style, however, tapping vernacular materials and reveling in its own composite character, could be fashioned to express the American condition, and, by and large, that was Bellow's aim as a stylist from *Augie March* onward. The entire volume of *Him with His Foot in His Mouth* (1984) crackles with this kind of stylistic energy. Shawmut, the narrator of the title story, notes of

[1]Saul Bellow, *It All Adds Up* (New York: Viking, 1994), pp. 317–18.
[2]Bellow, *Him with His Foot in His Mouth* (New York: Harper and Row, 1984), p. 30.

an aging wealthy woman, "The diamonds on her bosom lay like the Finger Lakes among the hills" (p. 28). In another story, when the narrator meets a cousin after the passage of years, "He looked like Death's sparring partner and his cheeks were battered under his eyes" (p. 242) Time's weight on another cousin in this same story is registered in these terms: "Now all the geometry of her figure had changed. She had come down in the knees like the jack of a car, to a diamond posture" (p. 262). James Wood, in an essay that is a perceptive, concise discussion of Bellow's style, shrewdly observes that this image and many others like it exhibit a strong kinship with the deployment of fantastic figuration in Dickens's memorable caricatures.[3] (Wood makes an excellent case for Bellow's prose having picked up elements of Dickens, though one might add that in this instance "had come down in the knees" is a distinctively American-colloquial touch.) The street-language snappiness of this style by no means limits it to wiseacre wit because it segues so easily into finely descriptive effects (the "elegance" of which Bellow speaks in his interview). Here, for example, is the report of an airplane taking off from O'Hare on a winter day, from the memorable novella "What Kind of a Day Did You Have?": "The jet engines sucked and snarled up the frozen air, the huge plane lifted; the gray ground skidded away and you rose past hangars, over factories, ponds, bungalows, football fields, the stitched incisions of railroad tracks curving through the snow."[4] The effective-

[3]James Wood, "The Jewish King James Version; Saul Bellow: Not Exactly English but Biblically English," *Times Literary Supplement*, August 5, 2005, p. 12.

[4]Bellow, *Him with His Foot in His Mouth*, p. 16.

ness of this sentence is in part the result of the initial strong sequence of verbs—sucked, snarled, lifted, skidded away, with the first two exhibiting an exuberant indecorousness that derives from the colloquial style while also being vividly precise. The rhythm of the sentence then beautifully follows the experience of the take-off; and "the stitched incisions of railroad tracks" is a brilliant illustration of Bellow's use of metaphors drawn from unexpected semantic fields for a concrete realization of the object of representation. This is a vigorous, engaging style that, in part because of its vernacular roots, does not seem self-admiring or self-conscious, as, say, the luxuriant prose of John Updike sometimes does.

It is important, however, to keep in mind that the "accents" Bellow sought to introduce into American prose are far from exhausted by Chicago street language, the model of Mark Twain, and the precedent of Dickens (to which James Wood adds D. H. Lawrence as well). American writers by and large have been monolingual. Many in fact never actually learned a second language, and most who did attained no more than a formal classroom acquaintance with any living foreign tongue. (Expatriates like Hemingway are a partial exception to this rule.) Bellow, on the other hand, grew up with three languages and the rudiments of a fourth. In his immigrant home near Montreal, where he spent his first nine years, his parents spoke Yiddish. (His mother also read Russian, so at least the idea of Russian literature and language was present in the environment.) In school, instruction was in English, which of course Bellow would embrace entirely when the family moved to Chicago. On the streets he heard French, and that language, reinforced later on by a year in Paris, would remain with him. In an interview with the Rumanian novelist Norman Manea a few years before his death, he reported that he continued to enjoy reading fiction in French, adding, impishly, "I can read Proust in French with great *naches.*"[5] *Naches*, one notes, is the homey Yiddish word for satisfaction or pleasure—say, the sort of pleasure a mother feels when her son becomes a doctor, or marries a nice Jewish girl— and Bellow exhibits a kind of provocative cross-cultural wit in applying it to the experience of reading Proust's intricately elegant prose. Bellow, in becoming a master of American style, held onto an anchor in Yiddish, his mother tongue. He put it to literary use on one notable occasion in his vigorous translation of Isaac Bashevis Singer's story "Gimpel the Fool," which, published in the *Partisan Review* in the 1950s, introduced Singer to an American readership. A revealing anecdote conveyed by James Atlas in his generally irritating and sometimes unreliable biography is that when Bellow got word of his Nobel Prize, he was so excited that, running into his editor on the street in Manhattan, he babbled the great news to him in Yiddish.

Yiddish is an imponderable and oblique presence in Bellow's prose. An American writer, Chicago-grown, he never resorts to the kind of Yiddishized English one often detects in Bernard Malamud. When *Herzog* appeared in 1964, Irving Howe, in a celebratory review in *The New Republic*, whimsically proposed that, with the emergence of books like this one, in another generation graduate students of American literature would be obliged

---

[5] "Saul Bellow: An Interview," in *Salmagundi*, Summer–Fall 2007, p. 200.

to study Yiddish instead of Anglo-Saxon. This was, of course, a deliberate exaggeration: in *Herzog* Yiddish terms are introduced from time to time, not always accompanied by translations, but the language of the novel, alternately racy, pungently lyric, and intellectual, shows no direct reflection of Yiddish. Nevertheless, there may be something of the tonality of Yiddish, though not its syntax or idioms, that enters into Bellow's particular literary elevation of American street language. The narrator of "Him with His Foot in His Mouth" dismisses sentimental notions of Yiddish and stresses instead its character as a "violent unsparing language": "Yiddish is a *hard* language.... Yiddish is severe and bears down without mercy. Yes, it is often delicate, lovely, but it can be explosive as well" (p. 16). It is plausible, if not entirely demonstrable, that something of this uncompromising wit and energetic toughness enters into Bellow's prose.

Bellow also studied Hebrew from early childhood in a traditional *kheder*. Although most boys come out of this Old World rote-education institution (an Orthodox Jewish equivalent of the one-room schoolhouse) with no more than an ability to read the Hebrew alphabet and to recognize a few words, the linguistically prehensile future writer absorbed enough of the language so that late in life he was reading Exodus and Samuel in the original; and during his year teaching at Princeton in 1952–53, when Edmund Wilson was acquiring the elements of biblical Hebrew at Princeton Theological Seminary, the eminent critic would sometimes consult the novelist on passages with which he was having problems. Occasionally a biblical phrase in Hebrew actually surfaces in

Bellow's fiction, but, like other American novelists, he seems to have chiefly relied on the King James Version for reading Scripture. He first encountered it when he was hospitalized as a child with peritonitis and discovered in his hospital room a copy of the New Testament, which he began to read avidly. In the last weeks of his life, as James Wood reports, he had the King James Version at his bedside. One could say that, in contradistinction to Melville and Faulkner, the King James Version was something of an acquired taste for Bellow. He successfully cultivated an intimate connection with it, but it was not from the outset part of the cultural air he breathed, and so claiming the canonical English version of the Bible was for this child of Yiddish-speaking immigrants a conscious act of fashioning an American identity. There is a good deal of evidence that all his life Bellow, unlike the other Jewish-American novelists with whom he is often bracketed, continued to reflect on the Bible, mulling over its language and ideas. Here is a revelatory moment from the novella "What Kind of Day Did You Have?," when Wulpy, the brilliant aging art historian, considers what his life has come to: "Now he had touched limits on every side: 'Thou hast appointed his bounds that he cannot pass.'" This recollection of the Voice from the Whirlwind in Job is reinforced a couple of sentences later when Wulpy, this time quoting the Hebrew as well, invokes a phrase from Job 14:2: "Wulpy had had his intimations of helplessness (the Biblical 'appointed bounds' didn't count, those were from another life—the *yivrach katzail*, 'he fleeth as a shadow,' he had studied as a boy)."[6]

[6]Bellow, *Him with His Foot in His Mouth*, p. 142.

Although Bellow toyed with odd and even crackpot spir-
itualist doctrines both early and late, and remained something of an eccentric religious searcher all his life, he
seems to have thought of the Bible from what was essentially a humanist perspective. As he sees it, it is one
collection of texts, among several, that confronts us
with a penetrating and challenging set of insights into
the human condition. "We have to go back to the Bible,"
he says in the second of his Jefferson Lectures, "to Plato,
to Shakespeare, to see what man once was."[7] In his 1991
interview in *Bostonia*, he evokes his own experience of
having grown up in the aura of the Bible: "My childhood lay under the radiance (or gloom) of the archaic
family, the family of which God is the ultimate father
and your own father is the representative of divinity. An
American (immigrant plus WASP) version of the most
ancient of myths: the creation, the garden, the fall, Genesis, Exodus, Joshua, Judges. The Old Testament became part of your life, if you had that kind of upbringing."[8] The compact summary, "immigrant plus WASP,"
is shrewdly precise: immigrant, reading the Bible in the
original and imagining it as your people's direct legacy
(the intimately remembered Hebrew *yivrach katzeil*), and
WASP, the eloquence of the King James Version ("he
fleeth as a shadow") that is part of the general culture of
English-speaking peoples.

Relating to the Bible is not only a matter of remembering stories, ideas, and images but also, as Wulpy's recollection of the phrases from Job illustrates, recalling the

---

[7]Bellow, *It All Adds Up*, p. 151.
[8]Ibid., p. 321.

resonant language in which defining perceptions co-
alesce. In an essay on how contemporary American culture induces a condition of debilitating mental distraction, Bellow beautifully evokes the way in which certain
words from great works of literature, including the Bible,
touch something profound within us, enabling an illuminating concentration of the imaginative faculty instead of its dispersal:

> A small clue will suffice to remind us that when we hear
> certain words—"all is but toys," "absent thee from felic-
> ity," "a wilderness of monkeys," "green pastures," "still
> waters," or even the single word "relume"—they revive
> for us moments of emotional completeness and over-
> flowing comprehension, they unearth buried essences.[9]

As a prelude to the consideration of style and its biblical component in Bellow's fiction, I would like to consider the concluding sentences of a brief 1990 essay on
Vermont (it was actually written for a travel magazine)
that ends with precisely these two phrases from the
twenty-third psalm:

> When the birds awaken you, you open your eyes on the
> massed foliage of huge old trees. Should the stone kitchen
> be damp, as it may be even in July, you bring wood up
> from the cellar and build a fire. After breakfast you
> carry your coffee out to the porch. The dew takes up
> every particle of light. The hummingbirds chase away
> hummingbird trespassers from the fuchsias and Maltese
> crosses. Grass snakes come out of their sheltering rocks
> to get some sun. The poplar leaves, when you narrow

[9]Ibid., p. 168.

your eyes, are like a shower of small change. And when you walk down to the pond, you may feel what the psalmist felt about still waters and green pastures.[10]

The still waters and green pastures perfectly culminate that revival of moments of emotional completeness of which Bellow speaks in his essay on contemporary distraction. (Indeed, part of the appeal of a rural retreat seems to be the possibility of return to a biblical pastoral landscape.) What is equally important to observe is that the movement of language throughout this passage is strongly, if unobtrusively, biblical. Although there are a few brief subordinate clauses, the narration of a summer morning in Vermont is essentially paratactic, like the King James Version and the Hebrew, advancing through a series of simple sequenced utterances in which verbs are prominent: "you bring up wood from the cellar," "you carry your coffee out to the porch," "The dew takes up every particle of light," "The hummingbirds chase away hummingbird trespassers," "Grass snakes come out." Complications of figurative language are avoided, with the limited exception of the startlingly fresh "like a shower of small change." Above all, the strength of the passage derives from a studied simplicity of diction (note the verbs: awaken, open, bring, build, carry, take up, chase, come out, get), for which the King James Version is the great model in English. One might recall, among many possible instances, the grand austerity of the Flood narrative in Genesis 7: "and the flood was forty days upon the earth; and the waters increased, and bare up the ark, and it was lift up above the earth.

[10]Ibid., p. 251.

And the waters prevailed, and were increased greatly upon the earth; and the ark went upon the face of the waters." The sentences proceed in a paratactic march punctuated by the and's (a device Bellow emulates elsewhere but not in the passage just cited). The biblical writer revels in the repetition of elemental terms—earth, waters, ark—and reinforces the dignity of the narrative by using the plainest language instead of any fancy literary vocabulary—"the flood *was* forty days upon the earth," "the ark *went* upon the face of the waters." (The translators' choice of "prevailed" here is the sole exception to this adherence to simplicity of diction.) The lesson in the power of unadorned stylistic directness was surely not lost on Bellow.

My choice of the brief novel *Seize the Day* for a closer examination of Bellow's style and its biblical strand may seem a little eccentric. Denying itself the flamboyance that marks many of Bellow's books, *Seize the Day* is not, I would have to say, as engaging as some of his longer, less perfect novels. It appeared in 1956, just three years after the expansively exuberant *Augie March*, three years before the beguiling existential comedy of *Henderson the Rain King*, and eight years before *Herzog*, with its distinctive fusion of poignant sexual farce and wry philosophical questioning. The very point of *Seize the Day* is its conscious classicizing aim. Everything about it, from form to theme, is about limitations. The entire action unfolds in a few hours of a hot summer day within the area of a few blocks on Manhattan's Upper West Side, and the plot involves only a small handful of characters. The protagonist, Tommy Wilhelm, is a man who has painfully hit his own limits, three decades earlier in his life than the septuagenarian Wulpy of "What Kind of Day Did You Have?" Caught between an implacable estranged wife and a self-centered, withholding father, Wilhelm allows himself to be bilked out of his last few hundred dollars by Dr. Tamkin, a preening charlatan who exerts a fatal allure for him as a "reality instructor," the term used in *Henderson* for this kind of figure that recurs in Bellow's fiction. *Seize the Day*, then, is about a hapless man trapped in the middle of his life, and it has a deliberately constricting quality, the only outlet in the book being Wilhelm's cathartic rush of tears at the very end. But there is scarcely a misstep in the artistic realization of Wilhelm's plight, and this short novel allows us to see in small scope all the constituent virtues of Bellow's distinctive style working in concert.

Since I have stressed the idea of formal limitation, it should also be noted that, paradoxically, *Seize the Day* also exhibits the sense of bustling energy that is manifested in most of Bellow's fiction. In the second paragraph of the novel, the narrator, having mentioned the "vast population of old men and women" that lived on the Upper West Side in the 1950s, goes on to say, "Unless the weather is too cold or wet they fill the benches about the tiny railed parks and along the subway gratings from Verdi Square to Columbia University, they crowd the shops and cafeterias, the dime stores, the tearooms, the bakeries, the beauty parlors, the reading rooms and club rooms."[11] This device of the catalogue recurs frequently: "Patiently, in the window of the fruit store, a man with a scoop spread crushed ice between

[11]Bellow, *Seize the Day* (New York: Penguin Books, 1996), p. 3.

his rows of vegetables. There were also Persian melons, lilacs with radiant black in the middle. The many street noises came back after a little while from the caves of the sky" (p. 74). "From every side he heard pianos, and the voices of men and women singing scales and opera, all mixed, and the sounds of pigeons on the ledges" (p. 103). The celebratory catalogue ultimately owes something to Whitman, who uses the device repeatedly ("of the smell of apples and lemons, of the pairing of birds, / Of the wet woods, of the lapping of waves, / Of the mad pushes of waves upon the land…"). Here's an especially Whitmanesque moment just before the end of the book:

> On Broadway it was still bright afternoon and the gassy air was almost motionless under the leaden spokes of sunlight, and sawdust footprints lay about the doorways of butcher shops and fruit stores. And the great, great crowd, the inexhaustible current of millions of every race and kind pouring out, pressing round, of every age, of every genius, possessors of every human secret, antique and future, in every face the refinement of one particular motive or essence—*I labor, I spend, I strive, I design, I love, I cling, I uphold, I give way, I envy, I long, I scorn, I die, I hide, I want.* (p. 111)

Whitman is present here but, also, in the grand paratactic surge of all those and's, the King James Version of the Bible. (We will presently look more closely at parataxis in Bellow's prose.) And Whitman, of course, has his own connection to the Bible, especially to the Book of Psalms. But what are these urban catalogues doing in *Seize the Day*? The catalogue as a literary device is the rhetorical embodiment of the idea of abundance, of the rich multiplicity of things in the world, and hence it is deployed in many of the masterpieces of the realist novel from Balzac onward. Though this is a story of limitations, it creates a thematically significant dialectic between limitation and overflowing abundance. Bellow has been justly praised as a preeminent novelist of American urban landscapes, and he is clearly a writer who loved cities, but the narrator's celebrations of the teeming variety of the city scene serve a special thematic purpose here. Tommy Wilhelm, the trapped man, can see only the enclosing walls of his private house of misery: the vanished resources, the loveless father, the vengeful wife. Yet all around him, as the narrator reminds us in these catalogues, there is a world that bustles with life—the shops and cafeterias and tearooms, the fruits and vegetables, the cacophonous symphony of urban sounds, the great current of millions with their dizzying variety of individual fates. It is an abundance of life Wilhelm cannot take in, a day he cannot seize. Between the protagonist in the foreground and the city in the background there is an antiphony of dead-end bleakness over against the hopefulness of life's continuing abundance and variety.

The reality of the circumambient world is repeatedly made vivid in the novel not just through catalogues but through Bellow's keen eye for concrete detail that becomes revelatory through the freshness and precision of word choice. At breakfast in the residential hotel where both Wilhelm and his father live: "Small hoops of brilliance were cast by the water glasses on the white tablecloth, despite a faint murkiness in the sunshine. It was early summer, and the long window was turned inward;

a moth was on the pane; the putty was broken and the white enamel on the frames was streaming with wrinkles" (pp. 17–18). "The light was dusky, splotched with red underfoot; green, the leather furniture; yellow, the indirect lighting" (p. 53). "[Dr. Tamkin's] amazing eyes had some of the rich dryness of a brown fur. Innumerable crystalline hairs or spicules of light glittered in their bold surfaces" (p. 65). On upper Broadway, one sees "a false air of gas... spurted from the bursting buses," while up above, "Light as a locust, a helicopter bringing mail from Newark Airport to La Guardia sprang over the city in a long leap" (p. 70). All these vivifying perceptions, of course, are the narrator's, not Tommy Wilhelm's, though a good deal of space is also devoted to tracking his troubled thoughts.

One should add that this stylistic gift for giving us the arresting appearance of things and people is sometimes implemented through the strategy of Dickensian caricature pointed out by James Wood. Of Wilhelm's father the narrator observes, "The old doctor's face had a wholesome reddish and almost translucent color, like a ripe apricot" (p. 34). Another item from the greengrocer's shelf is used to depict Mr. Rappaport, the aged investor Wilhelm encounters at the brokerage office: "Purple stains were buried in the flesh of his nose and the cartilage of his ear was twisted like a cabbage heart" (p. 82). Even the dust in the air of "the carnival of the street" is represented through Dickensian fantastication: "the dust going around like a woman on stilts" (p. 74).

This efflorescence of figuration does not, as one might imagine, lead to any kind of florid literary diction. On the contrary, Bellow consistently grounds his exuberant similes and metaphors in plain language: "In full tumult the great afternoon current raced for Columbus Circle, where the mouth of midtown stood open and the skyscrapers gave back the yellow fire of the sun" (pp. 95–96). What gives this writing tensile strength is its adherence to ordinary terms where the temptation to use fancy literary language might beckon. This is especially evident in the verbs. Bellow does not say that the mouth of midtown *gaped* or *yawned* but quite simply that it *stood open*. The skyscrapers do not, let us say, *reflect the sun's effulgence* but rather *gave back the yellow fire of the sun*. These choices are not exactly vernacular but have a kind of homespun simplicity and dignity, like the style of ancient Hebrew narrative as it is for the most part justly represented in the King James Version—"and the ark went upon the face of the waters." (James Wood has aptly noticed this particular stylistic affinity between Bellow's prose and the scriptural model.) Here is another brief instance in which the plain verbs do the yeoman's work of descriptive narration: "The traffic seemed to *come down* Broadway out of the sky, where the hot spokes of the sun *rolled* from the south. Hot, strong odors *rose* from the subway grating in the street" (p. 96, italics added).

Style is the great agent of transformation in the constructed worlds of novels. Melville's Shakespearian-Miltonic-biblical style elevates the motley crew and crazed captain of a nineteenth-century commercial whaler into the indelible actors of a cosmic drama. Faulkner's serpentine prose, with its recondite diction and its biblical lexical keys, transmutes a Southern family's catastrophe into an archetypal story of overweening ambition, primal sin, and the unending obsessional memory of historical trauma. Bellow's writing is pitched more toward making the palpability of the here and now imaginatively available. This is an aim it shares with the Hebrew Bible, though of course Bellow's descriptive impulse is not part of the literary project of the biblical writers. What he does have in common with them is a desire to present the narrative data in ways that allow them to speak for themselves, without a sense of elaborate literary mediation, without an obtrusive feeling of language calling attention to itself. I do not mean to claim that he was consciously imitating the Bible in this project but simply that he had internalized something of its dignified, even stark, simplicity of diction.

Let me offer a last instance of this use of language from a moment just before the end of the book that is a climactic revelation for Tommy Wilhelm. He has stumbled into a chapel where he finds himself in a line of mourners filing past an open coffin:

> The dead man was gray-haired. He had two large waves of gray hair at the front. But he was not old. His face was long, and he had a bony nose, slightly, delicately twisted. His brows were raised as though he had sunk into the final thought. Now at last he was with it, after the end of all distractions, and when his flesh was no longer flesh. (p. 113)

In the Bible, there is not a single instance of such a description of a dead body—or, for that matter, of a live one, since biblical narrative achieves its ends with no more than brief occasional attention to what the eye catches in the appearance of things. Here is a characteristic instance of how the end of a life is reported in biblical narrative: "And when Jacob had made an end of commanding his sons, he gathered up his feet into the bed, and yielded up the ghost, and was gathered unto his people" (Genesis 50:33). (The Hebrew, it should be said, is even more uncompromisingly paratactic. Here is my own translation, which replicates the Hebrew syntax: "And Jacob finished charging his sons, and he gathered his feet into the bed, and he breathed his last, and was gathered to his kinfolk.") Where Bellow's modern death is, as one would expect, individualized—the two large waves of gray hair, the long face and nose—the biblical death is traditional and, one might say, stereotypical— the last charge of the father to his sons, the gathering of the feet into the bed, giving up the ghost, and, as the living person turns into a memory, the joining of the dead man with all the generations of his kinfolk. What the two texts share is an unblinking gaze at life's end that excludes all melodramatic flourishes, all hints of pathos or sentimentality. Parataxis serves as a vehicle of this gaze, enabling a series of terse factual notations of the appearance of the corpse in the one instance and the final gestures of the dying man in the other. The biblical parataxis works through a single sentence of four sequenced verbs, each preceded by "and"; Bellow's parataxis involves a series of short sentences in which there is only minimal syntactic complication. The narrator of *Seize the Day*, filtering Tommy Wilhelm's perception through his own language, brings his protagonist face to face with what a person looks like when he has come to his irrevocable end. That final vision confronts Wilhelm, after all his confused scurrying about in search of a golden key to release himself from the imprisoning shambles of his life, with an existential absolute. The expression on the face of the corpse looks to Wilhelm "as though he had sunk into the final thought." The use of the definite article for "final thought" is worth noting: it is as though each man, as his life ends, plunged into the final thought that might be a summary or synthesis of what it has all been about. This would amount to a kind of internalized equivalent of the biblical report of death in which a set of universal gestures is registered as the person dies. The vernacular simplicity of "Now at last he was with it" gets it just right for this unadorned encounter with the ultimate truth. The dead man's freedom from "distractions" is a liberation from the very thing that has confounded Wilhelm (and that Bellow in the essay from which I have quoted identifies as a pervasive malady of contemporary American society). The concluding clause here then assumes a genuinely biblical dignity and power: "and when his flesh was no longer flesh." "Flesh," as we saw repeatedly in Faulkner, is a biblical synecdoche for "life." The repetition itself is biblical, as in "This *is* now bone of my bones, and flesh of my flesh" (Genesis 2:23). This terse sequence of monosyllabic words ("longer" is the one limited exception), insisting on the primary term "flesh," is a strong statement of Wilhelm's confrontation with the ultimate moment of a human life. It participates in the Hebrew Bible's uncompromising vision of the hard facts of existence: after all the travails of a person's life (the life of biblical Jacob abounds in them), flesh, with the animating life-breath now absent, becomes only the last simulacrum of flesh.

The recurrence of paratactic sequences in *Seize the Day* merits further reflection. Again and again, narrative data or the chain of the character's thoughts are conveyed through a series of short, syntactically parallel sentences. Here, for example, from the early pages of the novel, is the report of Wilhelm's abandoned education. Although the point of view is evidently his, as we infer from the one clear reference to his feelings, "This was another sore point," little effort is made to imitate the language of the character's unspoken thoughts, as it would be in conventional free indirect discourse, because the steady focus is on the plain facts of Wilhelm's personal history, registered one after the other:

> Wilhelm respected the truth, but he could lie and one of the things he lied often about was his education. He said he was an alumnus of Penn State; in fact he had left school before his sophomore year was finished. His sister Catherine had a B.S. degree. Wilhelm's late mother was a graduate of Bryn Mawr. He was the only member of the family who had no education. This was another sore point. His father was ashamed of him. (p. 10)

The artfulness of biblical parataxis is precisely in its refusal to spell out causal connections, to interpret the reported narrative data for us. Something analogous often happens in Bellow's prose. His narrator does not, for example, say, "It was an implicit reproach to Wilhelm that his sister Catherine had a B.S. degree, and all the more galling to think that his late mother was a graduate of Bryn Mawr." Instead, we get an unelaborated report of the facts: the lie, the leaving school, his sister's degree, his mother's degree, his raw feelings about his lack of education, his father's being ashamed of him. The laconic paratactic style is devised to make

Wilhelm contemplate the ineluctable chain of events of his botched life without evasion or mitigating interpretation. This pattern occurs again and again: "He had decided it would be a bad mistake to go to Hollywood, and then he went. He had made up his mind not to marry his wife, but he ran off and got married. He had resolved not to invest money with Tamkin, and then had given him a check" (p. 19). Even when the narration moves into the representation of Wilhelm's inner speech, it continues to use this kind of sequence of short simple sentences that are syntactically parallel: "For what right had Tamkin to meddle without being asked? What kind of privileged life did this man lead? He took other people's money and speculated with it. Everybody came under his care. No one could have secrets from him" (p. 69). In the Bible, such paratactic sequences are characteristically used to convey the unfathomability of acts, motives, and feelings that we as readers are invited to contemplate and brood over: "And Amnon said unto Tamar, Bring the meat into the chamber, that I may eat of thine hand. And Tamar took the cakes which she had made, and brought *them* into the chamber to Amnon her brother. And when she had brought *them* to eat, he took hold of her, and said unto her, come lie with me, my sister" (2 Samuel 13:10–11). The Hebrew is even more unvaryingly paratactic than the translation because every clause and every verb, including the one that the King James Version prefaces with "when," is introduced by "and" (the Hebrew particle *vav*). The gaps between the paratactic utterances swarm with possibilities. Of Tamar's thoughts and feelings as she heeds her brother's command nothing is said. Is she apprehensive, frightened, blithely unsuspecting? Does she anticipate some overture to intimacy or seduction other than the brutal command, to be followed by rape? All this is left open. Bellow, writing a narrative more concerned with internal experience, uses parataxis to represent the gap between the registering of facts and the character's capacity to respond to them appropriately. Wilhelm has a perfectly clear line on Tamkin: the dubious doctor has no right to meddle in the lives of others; his own claims to privilege are questionable, he plays fast and loose with other people's money; no one escapes his unwanted solicitations, nothing is hidden from him. These factually correct observations are laid out in a series of flat declarations, never swerving into elaboration or qualification. What we get through this stylistic procedure is a dumfounding disjunction between perception and action. Wilhelm knows exactly what is going on, yet he is unaccountably mesmerized by Tamkin, immobilized by him, allowing himself to be conned into having Tamkin edge out from under him the last shaky prop of his broken economic life.

In *Seize the Day* these stylistic affinities of syntax and diction with the Bible are reinforced by occasional but significant echoes—or perhaps one should call them fragmentary recollections—of biblical texts. Sometimes these are attributable to the narrator, sometimes to Wilhelm himself, who, though a man of spotty education, seems vaguely to recall bits and pieces of the Bible. As a rule, the biblical echoes are stylistically integrated with the surrounding prose, but at one point Bellow flaunts the linguistic heterogeneity: Wilhelm, overhearing his father, out of sheer self-regard, lying about his son's income, reflects, "how beautiful are the old when they are doing a snow job!" (p. 11). The mid-twentieth-century slang expression "snow job" highlights through contrast the literary turn of the syntactically inverted "how beautiful are." That phrase recalls a particular memorable biblical text, "How beautiful upon the mountains are the feet of him that bringeth good tidings" (Isaiah 52:7). If the writer expected us to remember the verse from Isaiah, it would be with ironic intent, because the bringer of good tidings is a self-serving liar.

One biblical book is echoed several times in the course of the narrative, providing what amounts to a thematic punctuation of Tommy Wilhelm's desperate story. In the Book of Psalms, where psalms of supplication are the predominant genre, the speaker of the poem repeatedly complains that ruthless enemies encompass him all about, lay traps for his feet, seek his life. This sense of beleaguerment closely matches Wilhelm's feeling about his own life, and so the alignment of his language with that of the psalmist seems apt. "I was the man beneath," Wilhelm thinks. "Tamkin was on my back, and I thought I was on his. He made me carry him too, besides Margaret [Wilhelm's wife]. Like this they ride on me with hoofs and claws. Tear me to pieces, stamp on me and break my bones" (p. 102).

The image of being ridden is not specifically from Psalms (though it could easily fit into the biblical poems), but the psalms of supplication abound in representations of being torn apart or trod upon by enemies, and images of the bones shaken or broken recur often. "Many bulls have compassed me: strong *bulls* of Bashan have beset me round.... I am poured out like water, and all my bones are out of joint" (Psalm 22:12, 14). "For my days are consumed like smoke, and my bones are burned as an hearth" (Psalm 102:3). "*As* with a sword in my bones, my enemies reproach me" (Psalm 42:10). (The Hebrew, which Bellow might well have known, is more violent, saying "murder in my bones.") Even when Wilhelm has a momentary experience of inner quiet, recalling the little yard of his home in Roxbury before his life fell apart, the urgency of the psalms of supplication enters his thoughts, if only through negation:

> He breathed in the sugar of the pure morning.
> He heard the long phrases of the birds.
> No enemy wanted his life. (p. 78)

The desperate pleas for help in Psalms constantly invoke "those who seek my life" (*mevaqshey nafshi*). Although the King James Version often regrettably represents this as "those who seek my soul," sometimes it gets it right, as in "They also that seek my life lay snares *for me*: and they that seek my hurt speak mischievous things" (Psalm 38:12). Wilhelm is actually his own worst enemy, the ultimate cause of the disasters that befall him, but he has a paranoid sense that enemies, Tamkin and the estranged wife being the chief instances, are conspiring against him, and this sense perfectly accords with the psalmist's reiterated vision of being persecuted by malicious foes. In Psalms, again and again, the terrors of imminent death are represented as drowning. Sometimes this is a metaphor for grave illness; often, it is a figure for the dire threat of those implacable enemies: "I sink in deep mire, where *there is* no standing: I am come into deep waters, where the floods overflow me" (Psalm 69:2). This imagery, too, infiltrates the language that Wilhelm speaks to himself: "But what have I let myself in for? The waters of the earth are going to roll over me" (p. 73).

These biblical echoes work so well in Bellow's prose precisely because they are scarcely felt as citations. Instead, one senses an affinity of outlook and feeling between Wilhelm's world and the Bible that from time to time surfaces in an image or turn of phrase which is just barely perceptible as biblical and yet is perfectly continuous with the vigorous modern language of this novel. Near the end, Wilhelm has a phone conversation with his wife. Hearing the harsh, unyielding tone of her voice, he is led to think, in the midst of the conversation, "She prided herself on being fair-minded. We could not bear, he thought, to know what we do. Even though blood is spilled. Even though the breath of life is taken from someone's nostrils. This is the way of the weak; quiet and fair. And then smash! They smash!" There is nothing spectacular about these characteristic sentences but they exhibit a quietly effective strength. The unadorned diction, and the paratactic series of short sentences (here also making prominent use of repetition) are stylistic features we observed earlier. Spilling blood is a universal image, though it, too, is a reiterated notion in Psalms, as, for example, "and shed innocent blood, *even* the blood of their sons and of their daughters" (Psalm 106: 34). The breath of life in the nostrils is, of course, an explicitly biblical idea. Taken together with the shedding of blood, it gives Wilhelm's reflections on his vengeful wife a biblical solemnity, or perhaps one should say that it might suggest an ironic discrepancy between the starkness of the biblical locutions and his rather extreme construction of his wife's actions. Finally, the colloquial abruptness of "And then smash! They smash!" (p. 108) not only expresses Wilhelm's sense of being devastated by his wife's hostility but also effects another alignment with the psalms of supplication, in which implacable enemies smash, shatter, break, trample on the vulnerable supplicant.

One of the rare moments in the book when Wilhelm manages briefly to escape the confines of his preoccupation with himself features no recollection of any particular biblical text or stylistic pattern but an invocation of biblical terms of spirituality. It also has, leavening the spiritual gravity, a comic aspect.

> He was going through an underground corridor, a place he had always hated and hated more than ever now. On the walls between the advertisements were words in chalk: "Sin no more," and "Do not eat pig," he had particularly noticed. And in the dark tunnel, in the haste, heat, and darkness which disfigure and make freaks and fragments of nose and eyes and teeth, all of a sudden, unsought, a general love for all these imperfect and lurid-looking people burst out of Wilhelm's breast. He loved them. One and all, he passionately loved them. He was imperfect and disfigured himself, but what difference did that make if he was united with them by this blaze of love? And as he walked he began to say, "Oh my brothers—my brothers and my sisters," blessing them all as well as himself.[36]

The injunction to "Sin no more" could have been scrawled by a fervently evangelical Christian, but "Do not eat pig" invokes a prohibition addressed to Jews and raises the question of Wilhelm's somewhat elusive Jewish identity. Given the almost complete absence of ritual observance in his life, this chalked imperative amounts to a little joke. The commodity in which Wilhelm is disastrously trading through Tamkin's bad advice is lard. (Bellow may well have been remembering Joyce's irony in sending Bloom off to the pork butcher, where the ambiguous yet archetypal Jew comes across a newspaper advertisement for a project of Zionist settlement.) At the beginning of the novel, there is scant indication that Wilhelm is a Jew. His last name sounds German, and his father's last name, Adler, could go either way. Then we learn that he invented the first name Tommy in his abortive attempt at a Hollywood career, adopting his given name as his last. Behind the Germanic Wilhelm stands a homey Yiddish name: "Might the name of his true soul," he wonders at one point, "be the one by which his old grandfather had called him—Velvel?" (pp. 80–81). Although Wilhelm's interactions during the few hours in which the events of the novel unfold are limited to Jews—Tamkin, old Mr. Rappaport, a Mr. Perls encountered at breakfast, and his father—there is no sense of belonging to any Jewish community or of attachment to any sustaining framework of Jewish ritual. Wilhelm does think back on going to the cemetery for his mother's burial and hiring someone to recite *El Malei Raḥamim*, the prayer for the dead, from which he even recalls a couple of key phrases in Hebrew. This memory, however, serves mainly as foreshadowing of the funeral—perhaps a Christian funeral, though this is unclear—he stumbles into at the end, where he will experience a cathartic flood of emotion. The rites, we may infer, by which we solemnly mark the limits of an individual life are universal and on some level interchangeable. The vocabulary with which Wilhelm struggles to define his own flailing spiritual condition is alternately biblical, Jewish, Christian, and, in Tamkin's dubious reality lessons, philosophic-psychotherapeutic.

Yet what distinguishes Bellow from most of his contemporaries among American novelists is that the protagonist's struggle is ultimately conceived as a spiritual one. (In this, he is linked to Marilynne Robinson, whom we will consider in the next chapter.) Wilhelm's experience in the underground corridor is fleeting, and perhaps for that reason it could be seen as self-deluding, but it is a moment of genuine access of empathy for miserable humankind. Contemplating the distorted and fragmentary images in the tunnel, he thinks of his own human image, bruised and misshapen by life and by the perversities of his own character, and a warm impulse of fraternal love—the possibility of accepting both himself and all these people—surges within him. This intimation of redemptive compassion for the wretched of the earth is probably more rooted in the New Testament than in the Old, but, in any case, Wilhelm's spiritual vocabulary throughout the book, as we have noted, is distinctly anthological. The language of blessing with which this passage emphatically concludes goes back to a whole series of texts in the Hebrew Bible, where the idea of blessing is uniquely prized and where the verb "to bless," as in this passage, is used both transitively and reflexively. Thus, in God's first speech to Abraham: "I will bless thee, and make thy name great; and thou shalt be a blessing:... and in thee shall all families of the earth be blessed" (Genesis: 12:2–3). The language of the

Bible, intermittently weaving its way in and out of Wilhelm's thoughts, holds out a tantalizing possibility—that a man might turn his life into a blessing for himself and for others, in contrast to the compounding of misstep with misery that this bumbling figure has thus far made of his own life.

The hybrid character of Bellow's style, which I highlighted at the outset, is linked to an awareness of a problem of multiplicity of languages that complicates the existential quandary of his protagonist. This multiplicity runs both horizontally, across the whole spectrum of people surrounding Tommy Wilhelm, and vertically, back through the strata of time to the literary beginnings of our culture. Wilhelm reflects:

> Every other man spoke a language entirely his own, which he had figured out by private thinking; he had his own ideas and peculiar ways. If you wanted to talk about a glass of water, you had to start back with God creating the heavens and earth; the apple; Abraham; Moses and Jesus; Rome; the Middle Ages; gunpowder; the Revolution; back to Newton; up to Einstein; then war and Lenin and Hitler. After reviewing this and getting it all straight again you could proceed to talk about a glass of water. "I'm fainting, please get me a little water." You were lucky even then to make yourself understood. (p. 68)

All this is a little wacky, and perhaps not merely on the surface. Yet the whimsical route back from the glass of water to the first verse of Genesis and Adam and Eve also has a certain justification that is connected with the artful amalgam of Bellow's prose. Wilhelm is no intellectual, but, like so many of Bellow's protagonists, he has a mind that worries away at the nature of things, pondering their metaphysical grounds, figuring them out "by private thinking." The glass of water is no doubt Wilhelm's exhibit A in puzzling over the problem of language's referential and communicative functions, or dysfunctions—like the exemplary table routinely invoked when anybody tries to explain Plato's ontology. It is also likely to make us think of the water glasses casting "small hoops of brilliance" on the breakfast table that Bellow's deft language evokes so strikingly. The words we ostensibly share mean somewhat different things to different people, and that is part of Wilhelm's problem in talking about a glass of water. But the words also carry with them a complex burden of history, one that even crosses linguistic barriers—as, say, from ancient Hebrew to modern English—and so there is no way of using them innocently, without reckoning with their past. This inescapability of the linguistic past is precisely what makes the general presence of the King James Version in American prose so deeply interesting.

The linguistic complications in talking about an ordinary glass of water, or about anything else, lead back to the vivid hybridity of Bellow's prose that makes him the most satisfyingly rich stylist among American novelists in the generation after Faulkner. He is a writer urgently engaged in the tones and moods and feeling of contemporary urban experience, chiefly Chicago and New York. To create an authentic representation of that contemporary world in his fiction, he needed to tap the vernacular register, the "street talk" he speaks of in his interview, and to find ways to blend it in with a more ample and subtle literary language. But whereas the vernacular changes with sometimes disorienting speed—almost nobody says "snow job" any more—literary language is intrinsically more conservative because it has a tendency to recall its own various antecedents, few of which become entirely obsolete even as history moves on. Bellow, a serious lifelong reader of the Bible in the King James Version with at least some intermittent reference to the Hebrew original, was finely aware of how the grand 1611 translation had made a difference in literary English and had provided a continuing resource for later writers. Against a trend in English prose from the Renaissance onward that cultivated lexical profusion, figurative ornamentation, and syntactic complication, the King James Version offered a model of spare diction and of a syntactic simplicity that amounted to a kind of studied reticence which generated its own distinctive eloquence. Bellow drew on this stylistic spareness as a fortifying counterweight to the exuberant side of his writing. In the specific instance of his characterization of Tommy Wilhelm, the paratactic terseness serves as an instrument for representing the fatal disjunctures in the consciousness of the character between knowledge and act. Creation itself had been narrated in a series of unadorned paratactic pronouncements, moving from God's speech to the creating of light, to the dividing of light from darkness and all the rest, and leading on to the water glass glistening in the morning sunlight on the table of the hotel dining room.

Reading the Bible, moreover, is not reading a style in a vacuum but a style that expresses a set of leading themes and a series of orientations toward reality. Thus

Bellow assumes that Wilhelm's sense of entrapment and desperation has a history, even more than the glass of water. Wilhelm may not be a reader of Psalms, but Bellow certainly was. And so the language used to articulate the anguish of this hapless average sensual man in the middle of the twentieth century harks back to the urgent cries for help registered in those Hebrew poems written more than two and a half millennia earlier: the mighty waters rise up to drown the speaker, enemies seek his life, stomp on him and break his bones. The biblical strand in Bellow's writing is not a scarlet thread that stands out, as it often does in Melville and sometimes in Faulkner. Yet, variously receding, disappearing, and reappearing, it gives weight and resonance to his prose. Perhaps this might be a stylistic resource in part suggested to him, as James Wood has proposed, by D. H. Lawrence, who came to the Bible from a British evangelical upbringing. His own interest in the Bible seems to have been fueled by his strong Jewish consciousness (despite the encounter as a child with the New Testament). But if he chose to have the protagonist-narrator of his breakthrough novel wave his American identity like a flag in his very first words, he sensed that this identity was characteristically expressed not only in an American vernacular but also in the pervasive presence of the English Bible in American culture, a rich repertoire of language out of which many of the terms of the national consciousness were framed. In drawing on the style and some of the imagery of the Bible, Bellow, as he also did in many quite different ways, was confirming the distinctive American stamp of his writing.

Chapter 5

୰

The World through Parataxis

When *The Sun Also Rises* first appeared in 1926, it seemed to many American readers that in it Hemingway had achieved a definitive expression of the mood and mind-set of his generation. The unmoored wanderings of his central characters first from bar to bistro in Paris and then across the countryside of Spain were felt to capture the bleakness and the inner devastation that for combatants and observers alike were a consequence of the Great War, and a prevailing sense of aimless circling and a quest for excitements destined to frustrate were perfectly encapsulated in the book's Ecclesiastean title. After the passage of eight decades, much of the novel looks rather flat—its characters sketchy, lacking psychological or moral complexity, and its plot a slender vehicle for development or discovery. Among novels of the 1920s, the *anni mirabiles* that saw the publication of *The Sound and the Fury* in America and the masterworks of Joyce, Woolf, Proust, and Kafka in Europe and England, *The Sun Also Rises* may appear a little anemic. It is a book that offers some confirmation for the often asserted judgment that Hemingway's finest achievement lies not in his novels but in a few of his best short stories—some of them compact narratives of only thee or four pages, for which his stylistic astringency is beautifully apt.

Hemingway's legacy, such as it may be, is precisely in his style. His fiction of the '20s, both the novels and the stories, and much of what he wrote later, have given certain American writers, from his own time to the present, and, through the medium of translation, some French and Italian writers as well, a new model of narrative prose, an ideal of tight-lipped artful reticence that might make possible a different way of seeing the world. The epigraph from Ecclesiastes that Hemingway chose, set beneath a six-word quotation from a conversation with Gertrude Stein ("You are all a lost generation."), has stylistic as well as the obvious thematic relevance to *The Sun Also Rises*, but the stylistic relevance has not been generally appreciated. It is, one should note, rather long as epigraphs go. The same thematic point might have been made with a more succinct citation of the biblical text, but I suspect that Hemingway favored the longer quotation from the first chapter of Ecclesiastes (close to a hundred words) both because it conveys a strong sense of the unending, pointless circumambulation that is the fate of his characters and because it carries us, before we have read a word of his own prose, into the cadences and swing and above all the syntax of the biblical writer. Here is the entire epigraph as it appears in the novel, including the points of ellipsis Hemingway decided to use to indicate the ends of verses in the biblical text:

One generation passeth away, and another generation
cometh; but the earth abideth forever... The sun also
ariseth, and the sun goeth down, and hasteth to the
place where he arose... The wind goeth toward the
south, and turneth about unto the north; it whirleth
about continually, and the wind returneth again according to its circuits... All the rivers run into the sea; yet
the sea is not full; unto the place from whence the rivers
come, thither they return again.

Although Hemingway does not quote the famous
"Vanity of vanities" that precedes this passage or the
equally famous verse that follows it—"The thing that
hath been, it *is that* which shall be; and that which is
done *is* that which shall be done; and *there is* no new
thing under the sun."—he could no doubt count on most
of his readers to make the connection, which may no
longer be the case in the twenty-first century. The English translation here is one of the finer moments of the
King James Version, eloquent in itself and hewing closely
to the contours of the Hebrew. The use of parataxis in
both the original and the translation is uncompromising: a steady march of parallel clauses, with "and" the
sole connective, and the only minimal use of a subordinate clause occurring in "from whence the rivers come"
(two Hebrew words, *shehanehalim holkhim*) just before
the end. The prose of the biblical passage is, of course,
incantatory, and this is not a feature Hemingway will in
the least emulate because his basic stylistic strategy involves a principled avoidance of the hypnotic magic of
language. The King James Version is also faithful to the
Hebrew in creating an English equivalent for the homespun simplicity and phonetic compactness of the origi-

nal, which surely was not lost on Hemingway. The Hebrew uses the most ordinary diction, and the majority of the words in the passage in the original are one or two syllables long. In keeping with this, the 1611 version on the whole avoids Latinate terms, the two most visible exceptions being "generations," the inevitable English equivalent for the compact Hebrew *dor*, and "according to its circuits" (here the feel and rhythm of the Hebrew might have been better conveyed by "on its rounds").

The epigraph from Ecclesiastes suggests that not only did the ideas of this heterodox biblical text engage the novelist, but the movement of language in the King James Version also spoke to him, intimating possibilities of how he might make his own language move in a way that contravened the established norms of prose style in the English novel. The process involved in Hemingway's emulation of biblical style is one that often manifests itself in literary history. If I may step up an analogy proposed long ago by the Russian Formalists, the literary iconoclast, in order to renew the instruments of expression, may go back beyond the model of his immediate forebears to a counter-model suggested by his great-great-great-grandfathers. Let us try to follow the operation of this process in a mode of prose writing that never occurs in biblical narrative, the description of landscape. Here is a view of the Spanish countryside in the Pyrenees seen from a bus as Jake Barnes and his friend Bill Gorton set out on a fishing expedition:

> Then the road came over the crest, flattened out, and went into a forest. It was a forest of cork oaks, and the sun came through the trees in patches, and there were cattle grazing back in the trees. We went through the

forest and the road came out and turned along a rise of land, and out ahead of us was a rolling green plain, with dark mountains beyond it. These were not like the brown, heat-baked mountains we had left behind. These were wooded and there were clouds coming down from them. The green plain stretched off. It was cut by fences and the white of the road showed through the trunks of a double line of trees that crossed the plain toward the north.[1]

As a syntactic vehicle for novelistic description, this passage, like most of Hemingway, is a vigorous departure from prevalent norms of English fiction, as I shall try to show momentarily through a contrasting illustration. Perhaps Hemingway would have devised this kind of style without having read a word of the Bible, but most literary innovations, as I intimated in my suggestion about grandfathers many times removed, build on unanticipated precedents. The diction exhibits a resolute simplicity for which the King James Version is the best model in English narrative prose. Note the use of abundantly repeated primary verbs, mostly qualified only by the prepositions that follow them: "came over," "went into," "came through," "went through," "came out," and, over and over, "was" and "were." (One could easily think of "the sun also ariseth, and the sun goeth down... The wind goeth toward the south, and turneth about into the north....") Figurative elaboration is studiously avoided, with the closest approximation of a metaphor being the colloquially ordinary "flattened out" and "was

[1]Ernest Hemingway, *The Sun Also Rises* (New York: Charles Scribner's Sons, 1954), p. 108.

cut." But the most salient feature of the passage, and the one that reflects the closest kinship with biblical prose, is the report of the landscape as one thing after another, without syntactical subordination. In the passage we are considering, this is in part an attempt to convey the effect of a landscape seen through the window of a moving bus, but the same procedure is used again and again in Hemingway when the observer is perfectly stationary. We are given a sequence of relatively short sentences in which the only conjunction in the sentence (except for the "that" clause at the end of the excerpt) is "and." Here is a striking illustration of a sentence constructed as an unswerving paratactic chain: "It was a forest of cork oaks, and the sun came through the trees in patches, and there were cattle grazing back in the trees." The pattern resembles a characteristic pattern of biblical prose, though in the Bible the object of paratactic report is generally a sequence of events rather than anything like a landscape: "and he rose up that night, and took his two wives, and his two womenservants, and his eleven sons, and passed over the ford Jabbok. And he took them, and sent them over the brook, and sent over that he had. And Jacob was left alone; and there wrestled a man with him until the breaking of the day" (Genesis 33:22–24). (Hemingway's decision to give his protagonist the first name of Jacob is probably biblically motivated: Jacob in Genesis 33 is about to wrestle through the night with a mysterious stranger who, though unvictorious, wounds him and leaves him permanently lame; Jake Barnes has confronted the angel of death in the Great War and come away with the lasting wound of impotence.) The effect of conveying the countryside through this paratactic sequence is to give us the landscape in its sensuous concreteness, uncomplicated by strategies of interpretation, which, for example, is what figurative language would do, and with no gestures of lyric heightening or sentimentalization, which, at least since the Romantic movement, landscapes have often invited: we get the road, the forest, the sun in the trees, the cattle, the plains, the mountains, the fences. The passage gains a certain strength through its very resistance to elaboration. This, the description suggests, is the hard, clear look of the Basque country on a sunlit day; we are put in touch with the immediacy of the things that make up the landscape, the plain language fending off any stylistic gestures that might presume to tell us what it all means or how we should feel about it.

To indicate how much this kind of prose diverged in 1926 from what had been the characteristic norm for descriptive style in fiction written in English, I would like to cite a rendering of landscape in the first chapter of Thomas Hardy's *Jude the Obscure* (1895). Hardy's novel antedates Hemingway's by three decades, but the kind of writing it exhibits continued to be employed by a variety of novelists, and, in fact, with certain adjustments, continues to be widely employed to this day. The passage is also useful to our purposes because it is not especially idiosyncratic: the mood, with its sober reflection on the cycle of the generations, is a Hardy signature, but, stylistically, the description is cast in the language that I will call standard-novelistic.

> The fresh harrow-lines seemed to stretch like the channelings in a new piece of corduroy, lending a meanly utilitarian air to the expanse, taking away all its grada-

tions, and depriving it of all history beyond that of the few recent months, though in every clod and stone there really lingered associations enough and to spare—echoes of songs from ancient harvest-days, of spoken words, and of sturdy deeds. Every inch of ground had been the site, first or last, of energy, gayety, horse-play, bicker-ings, weariness. Groups of gleaners had squatted in the sun on every square yard. Love-matches that had popu-lated the adjoining hamlet had been made up there be-tween reaping and carrying. Upon the hedge which di-vided the field from a distant plantation girls had given themselves to lovers who would not turn their heads to look at them by the next harvest; and in that ancient cornfield many a man had made love-promises to a woman at whose voice he had trembled by the next seed-time after fulfilling them in the church adjoining.[2]

What leaps out at the beginning of the passage, in strong contradistinction to Hemingway, is the promi-nent metaphor, which involves a layered interpretation of the represented scene. The figure of the corduroy fab-ric, however visually justified by the straight parallel lines of the plowed field, is a kind of conceit that elabo-rately mediates the observed object. Corduroy is a rela-tively modern fabric, notably manufactured in Man-chester, England's great industrial city. Because of its durability, in the nineteenth century it was especially used for the garments of working-class men. Thus, it is an apt vehicle for representing the fields as having "a meanly utilitarian air," deprived of their own long back-ground of history. That background, however, is then

[2]Thomas Hardy, *Jude the Obscure* (New York: Modern Library, 1923), p. 10.

abundantly supplied by the narrator (these observations are by no means Jude's), who, necessarily, has recourse to a lengthy subordinate clause ("though in every clod and stone…") to lay out the contradiction between what appears to the eye and the actual history of the place. Syntactic complication begins even before this clause, with the series of three participial phrases ("lending… , taking… , depriving…") that modify the initial subject. As the passage goes on, subordinate clauses are used both to carry the vision across space ("Love-matches that had populated the adjoining hamlet…") and through changing positions in time ("girls had given themselves to lovers who would not turn their heads to look at them by the next harvest"). In regard to these shifts in time, space, and attitude, the syntactic complication of the two clauses that constitute the last sentence of the excerpt is exemplary. What is at play in all this is a fundamental assumption of the realist tradition of the novel that in England goes back to George Eliot, to Jane Austen, and, before them, to Fielding: space and time are intricately intertwined; you cannot focus on one space without an openness to the possibility of considering other spaces contiguous to it or indirectly impinging on it or associatively linked with it; and time is not an isolated point but part of a continuum that invites shuttling between before and after. To represent this shifting system of interconnections, one needs a rich repertoire of syntactic subordination. In Hardy's case, a particular vision of the nature of human life is firmly imprinted on the description of the field, and, indeed, the actual physical contours of the field recede before the evocation of its function as a site of history. All those human energies

expressed, the bickerings and the weariness, the peren-
nial manifestation of desire fulfilled and often in the end
disappointed, become the real subject of the passage.
The plowed field is turned into the theater for a theme,
which is precisely what Hemingway's treatment of landscape seeks strenuously to avoid.

Before returning to Hemingway and his heirs, in order
to illustrate the persistence of this sort of hypotactic-
metaphoric representation of the natural world in British fiction, I shall quote just three sentences from a novel
published almost a century after *Jude the Obscure,* A. S.
Byatt's *Possession* (1990).

> The next day, when she drove towards Seal Court, the
> wolds were blanched with snow. It was not snowing,
> though the sky was heavy with it, an even pewter,
> weighing on the airy white hills that rolled up to meet
> it, so that the world seemed reversed here too, dark
> water above circling cloud. Sir George's trees were all
> fantastically hung with ice and furbelows.[3]

Here the point of view is the character's, not that of
an expatiating narrator. Her consciousness, however,
provides a complicating mediation of the seen landscape
and also has the effect of aestheticizing it. At the outset,
the wolds are "blanched" with snow, a bit of literary
diction that Hemingway (and the translators convened
by King James) would have firmly excluded. The scene
as the protagonist observes it is shot through with paradox, and syntactic subordination is required to register
this perceived tension: "It was not snowing, though the

[3]A. S. Byatt, *Possession* (New York: Random House, 1990), p. 156.

sky was heavy with it..."; the hills are airy, the sky heavy, contrary to ordinary assumptions, "so that the world seemed reversed here too...." The heaviness of the gray sky is picked up in the metaphor of pewter—an image drawn from a relatively valuable substance, unlike Hardy's corduroy, and hence nicely matching the metaphorical representation of the icicles in the decorative image of furbelows. Hardy, as we have noted, means to point a moral in his meditation on the scene. A century later, such homiletic flourishes are no longer in fashion among novelists, but Byatt does want to convey her character's distinctive experience of the landscape, which is a complex interpretation of it: snow does not descend, though it feels imminent; the usual valences of above and below are reversed; and the winter scene recalls both the dull sheen of an alloy used for household utensils and the festooned ornamentation of a woman's dress. This vision of a wintry countryside is by no means a momentous juncture in *Possession*, but it is characteristic of a general trend in the novel to deploy subordinate clauses, metaphor, and literary diction in order to complicate, interpret, and aesthetically shape the object of representation.

It is precisely from this trend that Hemingway's stylistic project is intended to dissent. Not to belabor the obvious, I shall cite only one additional illustration from the novel. In this case, the relentlessly paratactic style is used not to describe a scene but to report a sequence of acts, which brings it closer to biblical models. Early in *The Sun Also Rises*, Jake Barnes is riding in a Parisian cab on the Left Bank with Lady Brett Ashley, for whom he feels a lover's longing that he is physically incapable of consummating.

The taxi went up the hill, passed the lighted square, then onto the dark, still climbing, then levelled out onto a dark street behind St. Etienne du Mont, went smoothly down the asphalt, passed the trees and the standing bus of the Place de la Contrescarpe, then turned onto the cobbles of the Rue Mouffetard. There were lighted bars and late open shops on each side of the street. We were sitting apart and we jolted close together going down the old street. Brett's hat was off. Her head was back. I saw her face in the light from the open shops, then it was dark, then I saw her face clearly as we came out on the Avenue des Gobelins. The street was torn up and men were working on the car-tracks by the light of acetylene flares. Brett's face was white and the long line of her neck showed in the bright light of the flares. The street was dark again and I kissed her. Our lips were tight together and then she turned away and pressed against the corner of the seat, as far away as she could get. Her head was down. (p. 25)

The sole divergence from the strict sequence of parallel independent clauses and sentences is the one brief "as" clause ("as we came out..."). The first few sentences resemble the view from the bus we looked at before in offering a series of unelaborated images seen as the taxi moves through the streets of Paris: lighted square, dark street, trees, standing bus, bars and shops. The difference is that there is a freight of unspoken emotion weighing on the two passengers, and one may reasonably infer that the attention to the passing images outside is a tense or uneasy avoidance of that emotion on the part of both. The jolt that throws Jake and Brett together is a turning point; now he looks at her rather than out the window. The series of brief sentences and clauses in which he reports what he sees has a stroboscopic effect: hat off, head back, face momentarily lit by the light from the open shops, a quick glance outside at the roadwork illuminated by acetylene flares that also cast white light on Brett's face, defining the line of her lips. This last detail leads to the futile kiss, then Brett's physical pulling back and her posture of dejection at the end. The emotional power of the scene obviously derives from all it leaves unstated. This is the only moment in the novel when Jake actually touches Brett until his fraternal kiss of consolation at the end after she has left her young toreador lover. Because the decidedly unfraternal kiss here cannot lead to what it ought to, it is wrenching for both characters, but nothing of their pain is allowed to become explicit in the language. The emotional reticence of the terse paratactic sequence is, of course, a way of avoiding effusion or sentimentality. but it also engages us as readers in an imaginative interactive process with the laconic narrative report. We contemplate this sequence of images and acts stripped of all comment, uncomplicated by interpretive syntax or metaphor, and we construct Jake's desperate yearning and the mutual anguish of the two characters.

In this crucial regard, the prose resembles the biblical model not only formally, as unadorned parataxis, but also dynamically: it has an effect closely akin to the report of Jacob at the ford of the Jabbok—we do not know precisely what apprehensions or terror he may feel as he sends his wives and sons to the other side of the brook, or what may be going on inside him as he is accosted by a nameless stranger and is forced to wrestle with him through the night. As happens again and again in biblical narrative, the power of the moment inheres precisely in the terseness of the narration. It is a story, as Erich Auerbach memorably said, "fraught with background," in which there are large gaps of motive, feeling, intention, and meaning between the sparely reported narrative details—gaps that we as readers are invited by the very reticence to fill in. A similar process is repeatedly set in motion through Hemingway's understated paratactic prose.

One might argue that this technique eventually becomes difficult to sustain for the length of the novel because by and large the novel as a genre is a kind of narrative that works through elaborate specification and, often, minute analysis. There are fine moments in *The Sun Also Rises*, like the one we have just considered, but after a while a reader may miss the depth and complexity of character development one looks for in the experience of reading a novel. The brevity of the short story, on the other hand, often seems better suited to paratactic understatement. Let me cite just a few brief, thoroughly representative sentences from the beginning of "The Undefeated," a story from the 1930s. At the beginning of the story, Manuel Garcia, an over-the-hill matador determined against all considerations of prudence to fight again, has made his way up a flight of stairs to the office of a bullfighting promoter. An object on the wall catches his attention: "Manuel looked up at the stuffed bull. He had seen it often before. He felt a certain family interest in it. It had killed his brother, the promising one, about nine years ago. Manuel remembered the day. There was a brass plate on the oak shield the bull's head was mounted on. Manuel could not read it, but he imagined it was in memory of his brother. Well, he had been a good kid."[4]

This strongly realized moment is emotionally charged for Manuel and also ominously foreshadows what we can already guess is likely to happen at the end of the story. The observed image and Manuel's thoughts are equally stated in short, parallel sentences, the sole slight divergence from parataxis being the elliptical subordinate clause, "the bull's head was mounted on." The understatement of "He felt a certain family interest in it" is wryly ironic, and nicely conveys the character's hard-headed, unsentimental attitude toward death, either his brother's ("Well, he had been a good kid") or his own. These few sentences are also an impressive piece of efficient narrative exposition: we gather that Manuel is middle-aged—old for a matador—because nine years have passed since his kid brother was killed; we learn that he is illiterate, and we find out something about his tough-minded sensibility. Here laconic parataxis is used for free indirect discourse, taking us inside the character's head. Seen through the character's eyes, with no more than factual comment, is an iconic image that focuses the whole story: the head of a bull that was fought and that has killed.

The influence of Hemingway's laconic paratactic style on subsequent generations of American fiction writers has been for the most part oblique, thought intermittently it has made a certain difference. Its most direct

[4]Hemingway, *The Complete Short Stories of Ernest Hemingway* (New York: Charles Scribner's Sons, 1987), pp. 183–84.

carryover is probably in the stylized prose, so easy to parody, of the writers of hardboiled fiction, who had the model of Hemingway in mind but surely not that of the Bible. Indeed, Jake Barnes's initial description of Brett could easily be at home in a story by Dashiel Hammett or Raymond Chandler: "Brett was damned good-looking. She wore a slipover jersey sweater and a tweed skirt, and her hair was brushed back like a boy's. She started all that. She was built with curves like the hull of a racing yacht, and you missed none of it with that wool jersey."[5] But original writers do not often directly imitate the predecessors they admire, and "influence" is a somewhat misleading term for the relationship involved. For the most part, the role of stylistic and other formal breakthroughs in the unfolding of literary history is in the shattering of once-dominant precedents: an innovative writer demonstrates that things can be done differently, and those who come after go on to do things differently, more or less in the same direction but not exactly in the same way. *Ulysses*, for example, did inspire some writers to create an approximation of the stream of consciousness, beginning notably with Faulkner's *The Sound and the Fury*, which appeared just seven years after Joyce's novel. Stream-of-consciousness fiction has become increasingly rare, but the other great formal innovation of *Ulysses*, its break with the idea of writing a novel in a unitary style, its putting into play a wild variety of styles, continues to make itself felt, even if the heteroglossia of later writers is quite different from Joyce's. I would suggest, then, that Hemingway's adaptation of biblical

[5]Hemingway, *The Sun Also Rises*, p. 22.

parataxis to express a disillusioned and unsentimental sense of a harsh twentieth-century world opened up certain new possibilities for fashioning prose that spoke to some later writers. His stylistic project entailed a fundamental repackaging of English prose. Instead of representing the world through a syntax that was a vehicle of qualification, analysis, and temporal, spatial, and evaluative complication, as we saw in the excerpts from Hardy and Byatt, he showed how unadorned sequences of parallel utterances, as in the basic pattern of ancient Hebrew prose reproduced in the King James Version, could intimate strong feelings and fraught relationships. This precedent would be more directly helpful to writers who were themselves attentive readers of the Bible because it alerted them to how the sturdy, uneffusive language of the King James Version, eloquent in its simplicity, might serve the ends of modern fiction. Such writers are no doubt rarer now than they once were, but they still constitute a distinctive presence in American writing of a sort one is less likely to encounter in literary English written on other continents.

In order to bring this particular story of American prose down to the present, I would like to consider two novels written in the twenty-first century, Marilynne Robinson's *Gilead* (2004) and Cormac McCarthy's *The Road* (2006). Robinson has unusual credentials among American novelists in regard to the biblical background of literary English because, rooted as she is in the Congregationalist Church, she is a deeply engaged reader of the Bible—primarily, from what one can infer, in the 1611 translation. In *Gilead* there is an obvious concordance between style and subject because the narrator,

John Ames, is a preacher steeped in the Bible, constantly reflecting on its themes and its imperatives, as he tries to sum up for his young son, with his own death imminent, what his life has been. In those passages of the novel that are devoted to narrative report, one sees a strong affiliation with the paratactic forward march of biblical prose, most units of meaning linked by a series of and's, and an indirect affiliation with Hemingway as well. A single illustration, which by this point scarcely requires commentary, should suffice:

> We were up before daylight to milk and cut kindling and draw her a bucket of water, and she met us at the door with a breakfast of fried mush with blackberry preserves melted over it and a spoonful of top milk on it, and we ate standing there at the stoop in the chill and the dark, and it was perfectly wonderful.[6]

The rapid parade of parallel clauses and phrases has a distinct kinship with, say, the report of Rebekah at the well in Genesis 24, and it also is reminiscent of the kind of writing one encounters, for example, in one of the fishing scenes from Hemingway's early Nick Adams stories. But, in fact, *Gilead* is a novel in which introspection is more prevalent than narration because it is, after all, a book in which a spiritually serious person is trying to take stock of his life. The use of parataxis for introspection is an instructive instance of how far a formal device can be stretched because introspection is not much in evidence in biblical prose (one occasionally finds it in poetic texts in some of the psalms and, argu-

[6]Marilynne Robinson, *Gilead* (New York: Farrar Strauss and Giroux, 2004), p. 12.

ably, in Job). Here is a characteristic paragraph from the early pages of the novel:

> Well, see and see but do not perceive, hear and hear but do not understand, as the Lord says. I can't claim to understand that saying, as many times as I've heard it, and even preached on it. It simply states a deeply mysterious fact. You can know a thing to death and be for all purposes completely ignorant of it. A man can know his father, or his son, and there might still be nothing between them but loyalty and love and mutual incomprehension. (p. 7)

The little subordinate clause beginning with "as" (there is just one other in the passage) at the end of the first sentence signals the fact that what precedes it is a quotation from Scripture. The biblically literate reader will know that the quoted words are from Isaiah 6, which reports Isaiah's call by God to prophecy. That moment aligns nicely with John Ames's story because a prophet is a kind of preacher, and the terms that the Lord lays out to Isaiah indicate how ambiguous or self-contradictory the prophet's mission can be. Here are those terms from Isaiah: "Also I heard the voice of the LORD, saying, Whom shall I send, and who will go for us? Then said I, Here *am* I; send me. And he said, Go, and tell this people, Hear ye indeed, but understand not; and see ye indeed, but perceive not." In this instance, interestingly, Robinson is not following the King James Version but rather a literal pattern of the Hebrew, about which she may have been informed (she does not read Hebrew). In the original, the conjugated form of the verb is joined with the same verb in the infinitive as a technique of emphasis—literally, "hear ye hear," "see ye see"—and the "indeed" of the King James Version is meant to serve as an English equivalent of the emphatic gesture in the Hebrew. John Ames might plausibly ponder the verse in these Hebraically doubled verbs because he is said to have some knowledge of biblical Hebrew.

At this early point in the book, John Ames is puzzling over his relationship with his father, also a preacher, and wondering whether he might have been a disappointment to the old man. This psychologically and ethically complicated bond between father and son is not explored analytically in the bifurcating, syntactically ramified language that I have called standard-novelistic. Instead, the enigma and the tensions of the relationship are laid out, as in biblical prose, through a series of independent utterances, one thing after another. First we have the aching paradox of this relationship stated in insistent parataxis that is a direct borrowing from the Bible: "see and see but do not perceive, hear and hear but do not understand." Then we have a whole sequence of parallel statements about the internal experience of knowing and not really knowing: "I can't claim to understand that saying..."; "You can know a thing to death and be... completely ignorant of it"; "A man can know his father, or his son...." It should be noted that the diction here, unlike some of the biblically colored passages we have looked at from other writers, is not especially biblical, apart from the actual quotation at the beginning. Ames's language is on the whole American colloquial, an intonation you can pick up in "I can't claim to understand that saying" and, more clearly, in "You can know a thing to death." At the same time, he is an educated man who has done serious reading in philosophy and theology, and so the words he uses naturally move from ordinary American to a language of more abstract conceptualization, as in the glide from "loyalty and love" to "mutual incomprehension." It is a striking illustration of how the Bible's syntactic patterning can be used with a kind of vocabulary one is not likely to encounter in the Bible, and certainly not in its canonical English translation.

Ambivalence, the irreducible murkiness of feelings and motive and relationships, is one of the prime subjects to which the capacious and flexible form of the novel has proven itself admirably suited. One thinks of the very different and masterly treatments of this fundamental dimension of experience in George Eliot, Tolstoy, Henry James, Proust, and Musil. What is remarkable is that in *Gilead*, unlike the work of all the novelists I have just mentioned, this subject is treated paratactically. Here are a few characteristic sentences bearing on Ames's ambivalent relationship with his brother, who from his student years has put himself outside the fold of the church:

> I believe I have tried never to say anything Edward would have found callow or naïve. That constraint has been useful to me, in my opinion. It may be a form of defensiveness, but I hope it has at least been useful in balance. There is a tendency among some religious people even to invite ridicule and to bring down on themselves an intellectual contempt which seems to me in some cases justified. Nevertheless, I would advise you against defensiveness on principle. It precludes the best

eventualities along with the worst. At the most basic
level, it expresses a lack of faith. (p. 154)

John Ames is pondering here an ambivalence that involves his relationship not only with his brother but also
with the general society. A staunch Christian, serious
enough about his faith to question his own worthiness
as its vessel, he is clearly conscious of the great number
of people who in no way share that faith and may even
regard it as ridiculous. That sense of an existential challenge from the surrounding society is sharpened by its
manifestation within his family. He feels a fraternal
bond with Edward and respects his intellectual integrity
but sees the ultimate nature of reality in antithetical
terms. The way he chooses to carry out the exposition of
these conflicting feelings is through an almost unbroken
paratactic chain (there are just two short subordinate
clauses). What he gives us, or the young son to whom all
his words are addressed as a legacy, is a series of quasi-
independent assertions, each one strongly weighted for
contemplation and marked by a full stop: the resolution
never to say anything to his brother that would seem
naïve or callow; the utility of the constraint; the possibility that this posture could be a form of defensiveness
but perhaps useful nevertheless; the generalization about
the stance of religious people vis-à-vis nonbelievers; the
danger of mere defensiveness. All this amounts to a procedure for representing the discrete elements of a process of thought that is formally analogous to the way
biblical narrative represents the constituent actions in a
chain of events: one action is reported, then another
after it, and then another, with the burden on the reader

to work out the multiple, ramified, and sometimes ambiguous possibilities of connection among the elements
reported.

In order to illustrate how different this kind of writing
is from standard-novelistic style, let me recast the first
three sentences of our passage as they might have been
written by a mainline novelist: "I believe I have tried
never to say anything Edward would have found callow
or naïve, an effort that, necessarily, imposed a certain
constraint on me, though in my opinion a constraint
that has proved personally useful, for even if it might be
a form of defensiveness, that quality has not mitigated
what I persist in hoping to regard, in balance, as its utility." The sentence I have constructed may sound a little
like Henry James on a bad day, but I hope it will suggest
a characteristic set of stylistic strategies that mark the
dominant tradition of the novel, especially in English.
Once an idea is introduced, the complications and qualifications of its consequences are stipulated through a
series of syntactical branchings-out in explanatory or
analytic subordinate clauses. This procedure also has an
effect on vocabulary. When a narrator thinks about a set
of propositions in this way—for style is ultimately a
mode of thinking—he will need certain specifying words
to delineate the lines of connection between propositions. Hence, in keeping with the logic of my hypotheti-
cal rewrite, I felt it was necessary to add the explanatory
"an effort," the adverbial qualifier, "necessarily," and
the self-analytical clause, "that quality has not mitigated
what I persist in hoping to regard...." This general procedure surely has its virtues, and in the hands of a master like the real Henry James it can be the instrument of

the most subtle and searching illumination of character, motive, and moral dilemma. Robinson's paratactic rendering of introspection vigorously demonstrates that there is a different stylistic vehicle for serious thinking that has its own strength. I would propose a loose analogy with the distinction that the anthropologist Mary Douglas makes between the analytic thinking that is used by modern cultures and the analogic thinking characteristic of many indigenous and ancient cultures. Analogic thinking, Douglas argues, is different from but not intrinsically inferior to analytic thinking, and it has its own complexities, and consequently we moderns are not entitled to view it condescendingly.

Let me offer one final, brief example of the paratactic prose of *Gilead*, where syntax, diction, and an actual reminiscence of the Bible come together to produce a resonant statement about man's estate. It occurs near the end of the book, as John Ames wonders where all his reflections have brought him:

> Though I must say all this has given me a new glimpse of the ongoingness of the world. We fly as a dream, certainly, leaving the forgetful world behind us to trample and mar and misplace everything we have ever cared for. That is just the way of it, and it is remarkable. (p. 191)

The initial "though" is of course not a subordinate conjunction but a colloquial equivalent of "however" or "nevertheless." The only syntactic complication in these short sentences is the participial phrase, "leaving the forgetful world behind us." Ames adds to "We fly as a dream" the adverb "certainly" because he is referring to what he would suppose to be a familiar verse from Scripture that speaks of life's ephemerality: "He shall fly away as a dream, and shall not be found" (Job 20:8). The five words paraphrasing Job have the feel of an embedded quotation because, though the syntax of the paragraph is paratactic, the diction is not biblical. The matrix of the language is American colloquial (note the beginning, "Though I must say"), and this colloquial diction provides an apt motivation for the coined abstraction "ongoingness," which reflects a speaker of the American language reaching for a term that can express the idea of things going on and on in their own incessant momentum while each of us necessarily passes away. The emphatic triplet "trample and mar and misplace" is a slight shift toward a more literary diction as Ames voices a sense of pain over the world's intrinsic indifference to all we have valued after our inevitable departure. The final sentence, "That is just the way of it, and it is remarkable," is a full return to colloquial diction and intonation as the speaker, in perfect character as a Midwestern American, faces up wryly, and perhaps philosophically, to a distressing inevitability of existence for which not even Christian faith can provide full consolation. This moving summation of a man's sense of his life deploys a language that is not biblical, apart from the remembered verse, but some of its power stems from a biblical directness in the sequence of clauses and sentences, one perception following another in parallel structure toward a little climax of insight.

The novels of Cormac McCarthy are a fascinating case study in the operation of style because he is a writer whose mesmerizing power as a stylist often seems to exceed his range and insight as a novelist. The novels of the

Southwest border region that established his reputation (*Blood Meridian, All the Pretty Horses, The Crossing*, and several others) offer stories that involve the harsh and brutal initiation of young men, repeated acts of violence, and fierce vengeance. All this is done very effectively and at times can be quite riveting, but it also often seems a restricted field of human experience for a seriously ambitious novelist to cultivate. McCarthy's novel of 2006, *The Road*, exhibits obvious connections with his Border novels, though the setting and narrative premises are quite different. It is a future fiction that takes place some years after a global apocalypse. The unspecified general catastrophe is evidently not nuclear but incendiary: everything is burnt out, ashes are everywhere, choking the air and compelling the survivors to shield their mouths and noses with improvised masks. Small bands—and straggling individuals as well—of predators roam what used to be the United States, scrounging for remnant stockpiles of food and not averse to making their meal of any person who crosses their path. In short, after the destruction, the world has reverted to an appalling Hobbesian state of nature. The two main characters, who have not succumbed to the prevalent brutishness, are a father and his young son, both unnamed, like all the characters in the novel. The father's sole reason for continuing to live (his wife having put an end to her life early on) is to keep his son alive. That, in effect, is all there is to the plot of the novel. The consequence of this whole conception is that *The Road* is less a novel than a kind of fable. It certainly has power as a fable, whatever its homiletic insistence, but it provides very few of the pleasures and perceptions one ordinarily associates with reading novels. The anonymous father and son are emblems of survivors but are scarcely realized as characters. We know almost nothing about them apart from the father's constant urgent need to find the means to keep his son and himself alive, his repeated reassurances to the boy, and the child's anxious questioning of his father. The equally anonymous figures they encounter are no more than their functions—potential killers and one pathetic, failing isolate.

Yet, within its distinct limitations, *The Road* displays some remarkable writing. The basic challenge for the book is this: how do you use language to represent an order of reality fundamentally alien to the reality in which and for which our shared language has been framed? In the prose of McCarthy's earlier fiction, there was a strong thread of Hemingway's paratactic terseness interwoven, paradoxically, with something of Faulkner's more recondite and flamboyant language. In *The Road*, given the grimness of the subject, the background of Faulkner has receded, and the style repeatedly shows an affinity both with Hemingway's prose and with the related prose of the King James Version of the Hebrew Bible. Here, for example, is how the post-apocalyptic landscape is rendered near the beginning of the book:

> On the far side of the river valley the road passed through a stark black burn. Charred and limbless trunks of trees stretching away on every side. Ash moving over the road and the sagging hands of blind wire strung from the blackened lightpoles whining thinly in the wind. A burned house in a clearing and beyond that a reach of meadowlands stark and gray and a raw red mudbank

where a roadworks lay abandoned. Farther along were
billboards advertising motels. Everything as it once had
been save faded and weathered. At the top of the hill
they stood in the cold and the wind, getting their breath.
He looked at the boy. I'm all right, the boy said. The
man put his hand on his shoulder and nodded toward
the open country below them.[7]

Parataxis is the framework in which the landscape is
laid out: there are no causal or hierarchical relationships
here, just one detail of devastation after another as the
observing eye scans them, with "and" the dominant
conjunction and only the most minimal syntactic subordination allowed. Several sentences are merely noun
phrases without predicates, a procedure that here is ba-
sically a modernist extension of the logic of biblical
parataxis. There is a sole instance of figurative language
in the passage, "the sagging hands of blind wire," which
seems almost like literal fact in this ghoulish panoramic
view. As we have seen with other writers, the parataxis
is accompanied by a simplicity and phonetic compactness of diction, again with the King James Version as the
great precedent. The writing exhibits a preference for
monosyllabic words and clustered stresses: "stark black
burn," "burned house," "stark and gray," "raw red mud-
bank." McCarthy has a fine ear for the music of language, but it is an insistent, fiercely pounding music that
he favors. Lexically, this is a prose that parades simple
nouns, the direct naming of things—valley, road, tree
trunks, wire, house, hill, cold, wind. At the same time,
it incorporates small gestures that give it a hint of archaic dignity and perhaps strangeness. Thus we have

[7]Cormac McCarthy, *The Road* (New York: Vintage Books, 2006), p. 8.

"burn" in an older sense of "burnt-out place" and the deliberately elliptical and odd "save" to mean "save for being." The physicality and the taciturnity of "At the top of the hill they stood in the cold and the wind, getting their breath" sounds rather like Hemingway, as do the boy's scant three words and the father's mute gesture at the end of the excerpt. The panning view of burned house, abandoned roadworks, billboards advertising forever desolate motels, is also reminiscent of a characteristic Hemingway technique of reticence, as in Manuel Garcia's inspection of what meets the eye in the bull's head mounted on the wall. This is, in sum, a blasted world in which all ordered arrangements among things have been shattered, leaving the writer to register only a catalogue of instances of devastation, and in which any response of pathos would be false. Biblical parataxis, the sheer adherence to the report of facts in biblical narrative prose, and the related terseness of Hemingway's writing, become an appropriate vehicle for rendering this world. Notably, though the subject is apocalyptic, McCarthy avoids the high poetic register of the apocalyptic passages in the Prophets or the Book of Revelation.

Here is a characteristic instance of apocalyptic panorama in *The Road*:

> In those first years the roads were peopled with refugees shrouded up in their clothing. Wearing masks and goggles, sitting in their rags by the side of the road like ruined aviators. Their barrows heaped with shoddy. Towing wagons or carts. Their eyes bright in their skulls. Creedless shells of men tottering down the causeways like migrants in a feverland. The frailty of everything revealed at last. Old and troubling issues resolved into

nothingness and night. The last instance of a thing takes the class with it. Turns out the light and is gone. Look around you. Ever is a long time. But the boy knew what he knew. That ever is no time at all. (p. 28)

These grim sentences exhibit some of the same traits that we observed in the previous passage. Noun phrases in place of sentences—that expression of parataxis in extremis—predominate. Again, a hammering effect is achieved through the clustering of monosyllabic words: "their eyes bright in their skulls," and the last four sentences of the paragraph, in which the only word that has more than one syllable is "ever." The orchestration of sound patterns reinforces the feeling of tight-clenched prose: "skulls" and "shells" are an assonance that is also a kind of slant rhyme, intimating an interchangeability between the two terms; and the fine alliterative cadence of "nothingness and night" conveys a sense of bleak finality. There are two brief similes in the passage, "like ruined aviators" and "like migrants in a feverland," one expressing a sardonic discrepancy between the world before and after the apocalypse (no planes will fly again) and the other a macabre resemblance between the two worlds (the survivors in fact are rather like fugitives from a plague). There are also, in keeping with the laconic style, a couple of instances of merely implicit metaphor: the refugees are "shrouded up" in their clothes because they have become the living dead, and the same idea is implied in the choice of "skulls" instead of "heads" or "faces." The low-profile omniscient narrator allows himself a bit of terse commentary in the Ecclesiastean somberness of "The frailty of everything revealed at last" and in the remark on the disappearance of the class when the last instance goes. The diction as well as the syntax communicates a sense of truncation. "Shoddy" as a noun meaning "rags of wool" has been around in the language since the early nineteenth century, but in current usage it has been almost entirely displaced by its adjectival sense, so the reader feels as if something has been cut off. The fraught word "ever" at the end is another instance of cultivated strangeness. We would expect "forever," but that extra syllable might make it too much of a rhetorical gesture for this astringent prose that repeatedly tamps down language to its most compact units.

The boy's sober understanding "That ever is no time at all" points to another key function of parataxis in representing this post-apocalyptic world. In the quotidian reality with which we are familiar, we order time through a stable framework of memory and expectations, measuring it with clocks and calendars, anticipating and planning for what will come on the assumption, grounded in what has been, that in some respects we can exert control over the future. The intricate syntactic strategies of the novel in general, as we observed in the specimen from *Jude the Obscure*, provide the means for shuttling back and forth with semantic coherence between one time and another. In the world after the great devastation, this reasoned movement through temporal orders is no longer possible. The two main characters have only the precarious moment in which, often desperately floundering, they are alive: "The day providential to itself. The hour. There is no later. This is later" (p. 54). The paratactic march of brief sentences and sentence fragments perfectly conveys this apprehension of time as a sequence of discrete moments, each standing on its own, with no confidence that anything may develop through time or give it the aspect of a coherent continuum. In this regard, the biblical model of paratactic narrative prose has been turned to a purpose that is altogether antithetical to that of the Bible.

In *Gilead* the biblical background of the writing is pervasive. In *The Sun Also Rises* it is textually signaled only in the title and in the long epigraph from which the title was drawn. In *The Road*, that background surfaces briefly but quite significantly at just two points in the book. At one desperate narrative juncture when the father thinks he may be killed in the attempt to save his son from marauders, he reflects, "Now is the time. Curse God and die" (p. 114). These last four vehement words are of course exactly the words that Job's wife speaks to him (Job 2:9) after he has been utterly overwhelmed by all his afflictions. The global relevance of this biblical text to the novel is clear: the whole world has been savagely afflicted like Job, and the protagonist, unlike the biblical figure, is tempted to curse God, though he may also preserve a post-theological resemblance to Job in clinging to his "integrity" (the term Job's wife uses sarcastically) by not reverting to brutishness, by sustaining the notion, as he tells his son, that the two of them are among the surviving "good guys." The idea of cursing God points to a scary sentence that the father later pronounces to his son: "There is no God and we are his prophets" (p. 170). The explicit biblical echo here is from Psalm 14:1: "The fool hath said in his heart, *There is* no God." In the world after the apocalypse, the father, far from casting himself as a fool, is bleakly stating what an honest man has to conclude. Yet the ostensibly nihilistic idea that God does not exist "and we are his prophets" may undergo a dialectic reversal. There is no God in this burnt-out, savage world, but a father and son who try to sustain each other in love, who try to survive without becoming murderers and cannibals, might play the role of prophets of this God in whom it is no longer possible to believe. (The father's statement here is of course also shaped by "Allah is God and Muhammad is His prophet.") The stylistic affinity with the language of the Bible, "that old tongue, with its clang and its flavor," is never entirely separable from an engagement with the ideas and the imperative values of the Bible. Cormac McCarthy's fiction of a devastated future is meant to be a rigorous extrapolation from our troubled present, like many future fictions. Sentence by parallel sentence, word by hard-edged word, it draws on the structures and something of the diction of the King James Version to forge without pathos a reality whose harshness beggars the imagination. But the Bible itself, beyond its function as a model of style, also offers various possibilities of interpretation and argumentation for responding to an encompassing catastrophe, which is a phenomenon repeatedly envisaged in the biblical texts from the Flood narrative onward. The response in Job is moral outrage against the God who has so spectacularly failed to deliver on his own commitment to mete out justice to humankind, and Job's complaint, emerging explicitly at the one point in *The Road* that we have just observed, underlies much of McCarthy's novel. The response of the Prophets to actual historical catastrophe, whether imminent or already happening, was quite different.

The nation might be subjected to the most unspeakable horrors—its cities burnt to ash, its virgins raped, its young men slaughtered, the besieged population reduced to cannibalism, very much as in McCarthy's novel—but there was hope for a glorious restoration when all wounds would be healed and the exiled people again planted on its soil. Obviously, any such prophetic visions of all broken things made whole again would be a false note in *The Road*.

Nevertheless, the novel ends with an intimation, however qualified, of a possible restoration, and it is noteworthy that it is cast in theological terms of "God" and "mystery" (the very last word of the book). After the father's death, the boy is taken in and nurtured by a family that, like his father, has remained among the good guys in the struggle to survive, clinging to an unwritten covenant of integrity. The mother of this family actually tries to speak to the child about God, and not merely by way of negation. The boy's attempt to talk to God is unavailing but she tells him that this is all right. "She said the breath of God was his breath yet though it pass from man to man through all of time" (p. 287). Here at the very end, the background of biblical language for the first time strikes an affirmative note, with that background quietly marked by the decorous, slightly archaic subjunctive ("though it pass"), by the very idiom of the breath of God, and by the stately iambic cadence through monosyllables of "it pass from man to man through all of time." This contemporary imagining of an appalling end-time and what hope might be sustained after the apocalypse is anchored in the language and ideas of the memorable text that was put into resounding English in 1611 and first framed in Hebrew in the Iron Age.

These considerations of American fiction over the course of a century and a half should demonstrate that style in the novel is never merely a technical or "aesthetic" procedure but a way of imagining the world, of articulating value. The role of the Bible in the general culture of this country, despite the fervent adherence to Scripture in evangelical circles, has surely receded since Melville wrote his masterpiece in the middle of the nineteenth century. Though predictions are always imprudent, it seems unlikely that an American writer now could produce a novel like Melville's, swarming with allusions to the Bible, exegetically and polemically engaged in the biblical texts, approximating the cadences and verse forms and imagery of the Bible. The plain fact is that we no longer have a culture pervaded by Scripture, where Bible reading is a daily practice in parlor and in pulpit, where the active memories of ordinary people are stocked with many hundreds, perhaps thousands, of phrases and verses from the canonical texts.

Yet the fact that this story of the life of the King James Version in American prose fiction continues into the twenty-first century suggests that something of the old dynamic stubbornly persists. The business of making new literature is intrinsically conservative, at least formally, even when the writer means to be spectacularly iconoclastic (witness Joyce's *Ulysses*), because few writers want to turn their backs on the rich resources of expression that antecedent literary tradition makes available to them. English-speaking culture has been marked with a certain difference from other Western cultures because it has inherited a strongly eloquent canonical translation of the Bible that has to a palpable degree reshaped the language. (This may be partly true of Luther's German translation as well, though I suspect that its presence in German culture has been somewhat less pervasive than that of the King James Version in England and especially in America.) For the reasons I laid out at the beginning of this study, after the seventeenth century the language and the specific texts of the Bible made themselves felt throughout American culture to an extent that visibly exceeded what was observable in the changing cultural situation in England. This ubiquity of the Bible set the context for the creation of one variety of American prose—there were, of course, others—that looked different from characteristic stylistic practice in its British counterpart. Clearly, not all, or even most, American writers were drawn to biblical diction, syntax, and cadences, but there is a distinguishable biblical line in American writing that has not yet entirely broken off. What Edmund Wilson called the "concise solid stamp" of the language of the Bible continues to appeal to some American writers, and inseparable from the stylistic traits is a whole world of values with which both writers and readers have to contend—a demanding, often stern morality; a ringing promise of redeemed history in which it seems increasingly hard to give credence; a contrasting vision of the horrors to which life in history is exposed; a penetrating sense of the unfathomability of human nature; the belief in a benevolent, providential deity and a vehement challenge to that very belief. All this, as Wilson says, we can never quite accommodate. Yet some American writers have felt, and a few continue to feel, that their ability to imagine humanity and history and the larger order of things would be impoverished without the resources of language and thought that the Bible provides.

Let us end by going back to the beginning as it is rendered in the King James Version: "And God said, Let there be light: and there was light. And God saw the light, that *it was* good: and God divided the light from the darkness. And God called the light Day, and the darkness he called Night. And the evening and the morning were the first day." This is, of course, by no means a scientific account of the origins of the world, but it is a strong statement, cast in the stately paratactic cadences of the Priestly writer that are nicely echoed by the 1611 translators, about the nature of reality: all is harmonious; being emerges as a sequence of distinct oppositions firmly divided by the Creator and aptly mirrored textually in the balanced progression of parallel clauses. It is a grand, simple style that a good writer might be tempted to embrace or at least somehow cite. It is a statement a writer might want to quarrel with or reverse, as Robert Frost does in "Once by the Pacific," where the speaker, contemplating the raging chaos of the waves, invokes an apocalyptic "God's last *Put out the Light*" at the end of the poem. Faulkner, too, makes contentious use of these verses when he compares the creation of Sutpen's Hundred out of nothing—this overweening man playing God—to "the oldentime *Be Light*." The essential point for the history of our literature is that the resonant language and the arresting vision of the canonical text, however oldentime they may be, continue to ring in cultural memory. We may break them apart or turn them around, but they are tools we still use on occasion to construct the world around us. That is precisely what a series of strong American writers since Melville have been doing.

Index

❦